TWAYNE'S WORLD AUTHORS SERIES

A Survey of the World's Literature

Sylvia E. Bowman, Indiana University

GENERAL EDITOR

France

Maxwell A. Smith, Guerry Professor of French, Emeritus
The University of Chattanooga
Visiting Professor in Modern Languages
The Florida State University

EDITOR

Ernest Renan

(*TWAS* 34)

TWAYNE'S WORLD AUTHORS SERIES (TWAS)

*The purpose of TWAS is to survey the major writers
—novelists, dramatists, historians, poets, philosophers,
and critics—of the nations of the world. Among the
national literatures covered are those of Australia,
Canada, China, Eastern Europe, France, Germany,
Greece, India, Italy, Japan, Latin America, New Zea-
land, Poland, Russia, Scandinavia, Spain, and the
African nations, as well as Hebrew, Yiddish, and
Latin Classical literatures. This survey is comple-
mented by Twayne's United States Authors Series
and English Authors Series*

*The intent of each volume in these series is to present
a critical-analytical study of the works of the writer;
to include biographical and historical material that
may be necessary for understanding, appreciation,
and critical appraisal of the writer; and to present all
material in clear, concise English—but not to vitiate
the scholarly content of the work by doing so.*

Ernest Renan

By RICHARD M. CHADBOURNE

Professor of French
The University of Colorado

Twayne Publishers, Inc.   ::   New York

To

Larry, Eric, and Eugene

Preface

Writing this book has afforded its author the good fortune of returning to Renan after almost ten years away from his work. In an earlier study, *Ernest Renan as an Essayist* (1957), I approached this great historian, critic, and artist in words from the somewhat unusual angle of his essays; and this was for several reasons: my interest in the genre as practiced by French writers, the wish to reveal his neglected accomplishments in it, and my feeling that it was a key to the serious side of an author who for many has appeared, despite his Christian name, to be lacking in seriousness. I may, in fact, out of the commendable desire to restore balance, have stressed his *sérieux* too heavily. In rereading Renan and concentrating upon the great works I treated only briefly before—*L'Avenir de la science, Les Origines du christianisme, Histoire du peuple d'Israël, Dialogues et Drames philosophiques, Souvenirs d'enfance et de jeunesse*—I was challenged by the opportunity to give a picture of his achievement which would do justice to his earnestness and depth while not sacrificing his inimitable irony, his humor, his sense of play; a picture showing him to be both skeptic and believer, both lucid critic and persistent idealist—an "idealist without illusions," as the late President Kennedy has been called. (In Renan's case one needs to qualify a bit: "almost without illusions.")

The order of presentation, through Chapter 4, is roughly chronological. The amount of space given to the analysis of his youthful works (Chapters 1-4) is justified by the fact that he is one of those authors whose major ideas and themes, a long time ripening, are constantly being hinted at or foreshadowed in his early writings, before finding their happiest expression in his maturity. In Chapters 5-8 the treatment is more thematic than chronological. In Chapter 5, I discard chronology in order to survey the whole of Renan's major historical work. This is my central chapter, just as history was Renan's central and most revealing accomplishment. The writing of history for him, while retaining its claim to be partly a science, which examines an object of knowledge distinct from the self, is also a means of expressing his own personal dialectic, through what becomes a kind of symbol of his inner world. Of his essay collections I have said little in this book, taking the liberty of referring the reader to *Ernest Renan as an Essayist.* Chapter 6 does contain, however, a discussion of his political (in the broadest sense) essays and speeches, though from a different point of view than that taken in my earlier book. Chapters 7 and 8 analyze his other major productions—philosophical dialogues and dramas, and autobiography—in such a way as to reveal how they grow out of youthful roots.

The frequent flashbacks to *œuvres de jeunesse* throughout the book have a distinct advantage: they have enabled me, I hope, to establish an important feature alluded to by some of Renan's most authoritative interpreters (Mott, Pommier, Henriette Psichari), but needing to be demonstrated with more thoroughness, namely, the unity of his thought. Here again, I am grateful for the chance to amend my belief of a decade ago that his later works (roughly, 1870 to 1892) are disruptions or dislocations of his earlier ones, and hard to reconcile with them. I am now convinced that Renan's work as a whole is a continuity, a harmony (what he calls *eurythmie*)—though a harmony, paradoxically, of discordant notes (Chapter 9).

The edition used is the *Oeuvres complètes,* edited by Renan's granddaughter and one of his finest critics, Madame Henriette Psichari. In the interests of a smoother text and a greater economy of footnotes, I have refrained from providing precise references for all the passages quoted, but I have tried to indicate as often as possible the source referred to. When precise references are given, they are in terms of the volume and page of the Psichari edition. Translations are my own. Occasional French originals (especially of key phrases) serve to give the flavor of a style justly recognized as that of one of France's greatest prose writers.

Except perhaps for his biography of Jesus and his autobiography, Renan's works are less widely read today than in his own time. His ambiguous attitude toward Christianity and his reputation (exaggerated) for evasiveness may have something to do with his diminished influence. More significant, as an obstacle to the reassessment we need of his work, may be the contemporary taste for the so-called "tragic view of life." Renan persisted in believing, with the Greeks, that reason and knowledge provide the key to health and virtue; he also stubbornly held, with the

Hebrews, that the world can be made more just than it is. Anxiety and guilt were such repugnant concepts to him that he tried to remove them—along with the supernatural—from Christianity itself. His pessimism he qualified as "fruitful"; his outlook was basically comic. Such views have fewer champions today than they had in the nineteenth century. But Renan's faith in "rational and progressive humanism," and in the attainment of justice on earth (*Préface, Histoire du peuple d'Israël*), should at least be examined on its merits; it should not be so easily abandoned. If one has the impression, in trying to show his relevance to our age, of working against the grain, the fault may be less his than ours; if he is not what we want, he may be what we need. To arouse the reader's curiosity to discover him would certainly be a satisfying goal to achieve, for only Renan himself, in his works, can prove his meaning for the modern world.

RICHARD M. CHADBOURNE

University of Colorado

Contents

"To feel and to think, is the whole of man,
What he thinks and feels is his God."
(Sentir et penser, c'est tout l'homme,
Ce qu'il sent et pense est son Dieu.)

— Renan, at twenty-two, in
poem, *L'Idéal*, 1845

"I beg those of you who will see me but this one
time to preserve of me, when I shall no longer
be in this world, an affectionate memory."

— Renan, at sixty-three, in
speech to Association of
Students, 1886

Chronology

1823 Joseph-Ernest Renan born, February 28, in Tréguier, Brittany (Côtes-du-Nord); father, Philibert Renan, grocer and merchant-mariner; mother, Magdelaine Féger, assists in *commerce d'épicerie;* Ernest their third and last child; brother, Alain, had been born in 1809, sister, Henriette, in 1811.

1828 Philibert Renan fails to return with crew from Saint-Malo; his body later recovered from bay near that town. Accidental drowning? Suicide? Family left in state of semi-poverty; moves temporarily to Lannion, where mother's relatives live.

1832 Ernest placed in Ecole ecclésiastique of Tréguier.

1835 Henriette, unsuccessful in attempts to found private school for girls in Tréguier, leaves for teaching position in Paris.

1838–
1841 Ernest at Petit séminaire, Saint-Nicolas du Chardonnet, Paris. Studies rhetoric.

1841–
1843 At seminary of Issy-les-Moulineaux, near Paris, annex of Grand séminaire of Saint-Sulpice. Studies philosophy.

1841–
1850 Henriette in Poland as governess in aristocratic family.

1843–
1845 Ernest at Saint-Sulpice seminary. Studies theology.

1845–
1849 Abandons vocation. Tutor at Collège Stanislas, then at Pension Crouzet, Paris. Takes *baccalauréat* and *licence.*

1845 Begins life-long friendship with chemist, Marcellin Berthelot (born 1827).

1845–
1846 Writes *Cahiers de jeunesse,* published posthumously in 1906-1907.

1847 Wins Volney Prize for essay on Semitic languages.

1848–
1849   Conceives and writes *L'Avenir de la science,* published in 1890.

1848   Writes unfinished "novel," *Ernest et Béatrix,* published posthumously in *Fragments intimes et romanesques,* 1914. Publishes *De l'origine du langage.* Receives *agrégation de philosophie.*

1849–
1850   Carries out learned mission in Italy for government of Louis Napoléon; eight months of travel; writes second unfinished "novel," *Patrice,* in Rome, also published posthumously in *Fragments intimes.*

1850–
1851   Rejoined by sister in Paris. Begins collaboration with *Revue des deux mondes.*

1851–
1860   Employed in Department of Oriental Manuscripts, Bibliothèque Nationale.

1852   Receives *doctorat-ès-lettres* for French thesis (*Averroès et l'averroïsme*) and Latin thesis (*De philosophia peripetetica apud Syros*); revised and enlarged editions of *Averroès* published in 1861, 1866.

1853   Begins collaboration with *Journal des débats.*

1855   *Histoire générale et système comparé des langues sémitiques,* revised and expanded version of Prix Volney essay.

1856   Elected to Académie des Inscriptions et Belles-Lettres. Marries Cornélie Scheffer, niece and adopted daughter of the painter, Ary Scheffer.

1857   *Etudes d'histoire religieuse.* His first child, a son, Ary, is born.

1858   Named to committee charged with writing *Histoire littéraire de la France.* Translation, with commentary, of *Book of Job.*

1859   *Essais de morale et de critique.* Daughter Ernestine born.

1860   Translation, with commentary, of *Song of Songs.* Death of Ernestine, at age of eight months.

1860–
1861   Learned mission (in part archaeological) to sites of ancient Phoenicia (Syria). Visits Holy Land. Ernest and Henriette gravely ill with malaria. Death of Henriette in Amschit, 1861. On return to France, begins association with Prince Napoléon (1821-1891, cousin of Napoléon III), patron of arts and partisan of Liberal Empire.

1862 Appointed Professor of Hebraic, Chaldean, and Syrian
Languages at Collège de France. Course suspended after
controversial opening lecture. Private printing of *Ma Sœur
Henriette* (published posthumously in 1895). Daughter,
Noémi, born.

1863 Begins attending dinners at Restaurant Magny (with Gon-
courts, Taine, Sainte-Beuve, Flaubert, et al.). Publishes
Vie de Jésus (vol. I of *Les Origines du christianisme*):
ten editions by end of 1863, translations in 1863-1864 into
German, English, Danish, Spanish, Dutch, Italian, Hun-
garian, Portuguese, Russian, Swedish, Czech.

1864 Expelled from professorship and appointed Assistant Director of Department of Manuscripts in Imperial Library.

1864–
1865 Second journey to Middle East (including Athens); re-
traces travels of Saint Paul.

1866 *Les Apôtres* (vol. II, *Origines*).

1867 Founds collection of Semitic inscriptions (*Corpus Inscriptionum Semiticarum*). Named Secretary of Société Asiatique. Thirteenth edition of *Vie de Jésus*, with important
Preface and Appendix on Fourth Gospel.

1868 *Questions contemporaines*. Death of his mother; returns
to visit Brittany after absence of twenty-three years.

1869 *Saint Paul* (vol. III, *Origines*). Unsuccessful candidate
for deputyship in electoral district of Meaux (Seine-et-
Marne), for Third Party (proposing acceptance of Bona-
parte dynasty as constitutional monarchy).

1870–
1871 Franco-Prussian War. Travels with Prince Napoléon (Nor-
way, Scotland). Publishes exchange of letters with
German Biblical critic, David Strauss, on causes and significance of Franco-Prussian War. Upon fall of Second
Empire, reinstated in professorship at Collège de France.

1871 *La Réforme intellectuelle et morale*. Travels with wife in
Provence and Italy.

1873 *L'Antéchrist* (vol. IV, *Origines*).

1874–
1875 Completes publication of *Mission de Phénicie*. Continues
return visits to Italy.

1876 *Dialogues et fragments philosophiques*.

1877 *Les Evangiles et la seconde génération chrétienne* (vol.
V, *Origines*). In Holland to participate in bicentenary of
Spinoza's death.

1878   Elected to Académie Française replacing Claude Bernard. Second unsuccessful electoral campaign, for senatorial seat (Bouches-du-Rhône). *Mélanges d'histoire et de voyages* and *Caliban,* philosophical drama.

1879   *L'Eglise chrétienne* (vol. VI, *Origines*). Travels in France, Switzerland, Italy. Begins attending monthly Celtic dinners in Paris.

1880   In England for Hibbert Lectures (London), published as *Conférences d'Angleterre.*

1881   *L'Eau de Jouvence,* philosophical drama.

1882   Translation, with commentary, of *Ecclesiastes. Marc-Aurèle et la fin du monde antique* (vol. VII, concluding *Origines*).

1883   *Souvenirs d'enfance et de jeunesse* (begun in 1875). Elected Administrator of Collège de France.

1884   *Nouvelles études d'histoire religieuse.*

1885   Begins spending summers at property in Rosmapamon, Brittany. Named President of Société Asiatique. *Le Prêtre de Némi,* philosophical drama.

1886   *L'Abbesse de Jouarre,* philosophical drama.

1887–
1893   *Histoire du peuple d'Israël,* five volumes, of which last two published posthumously.

1887   *Discours et conférences.*

1888   Collected edition of *Drames philosophiques.*

1890   *L'Avenir de la science.*

1892   *Feuilles détachées.* Death of Renan (October 2), of pneumonia and heart trouble, in his apartment at the Collège de France.

CHAPTER 1

Between Two Worlds

RENAN belonged to a superbly creative generation of French-men who were born around 1820 and are called both the "generation of 1848" (since their coming to maturity coincided with the Revolution of 1848) and the "generation of the Second Empire" (since they produced many of their works between 1852 and 1870). His more or less exact contemporaries included the novelists Flaubert and Edmond de Goncourt, the poets Le-conte de Lisle and Baudelaire, the painters Millet and Courbet, the composers Gounod, Franck, and Lalo, the critic Taine, and the scientists Pasteur and Marcellin Berthelot. The latter was Renan's best and life-long friend. Perhaps the most striking single characteristic of the great writers among this generation is that despite an attitude toward life more critical, skeptical, and apparently more disillusioned than that of their Romantic predecessors—*critique, science, intelligence, méfiance* (distrust), *la peur d'être dupe* (the fear of being taken in) are key terms with them—they nevertheless managed not to be dwarfed by such Romantic giants as Lamartine or Hugo, Balzac or Michelet, to establish their own originality, and to emerge as creative geniuses in their own right.

Yet Renan had other contemporaries. The historian of art, Henri Focillon, in his *Vie des formes* (p. 76), writes: "Each man is first the contemporary of himself and of his generation, but he is also the contemporary of the spiritual group of which he is a part." Renan's contemporaries in this sense were as much Plato and the Hebrew prophets as Berthelot, as much Marcus Aurelius and the Celtic saints as Leconte de Lisle; he was as close to the seventeenth-century religious philosophers Male-branche and Fénelon, and to Herder, Hegel, and Goethe in the German Enlightenment, as to Flaubert. Indeed, the first signifi-cant fact to note about him is that, although he began life in the nineteenth century, it was only in the chronological sense. Spiritually, his roots were in the ancient episcopal town of Tréguier, in Brittany (Côtes-du-Nord), whose original founda-

17

tions went back to a sixth-century monastery and in which medieval and seventeenth-century forces were still what Focillon
would call "living presences." The first test of his mature strength
was to result in his discovery of the nineteenth century and of
the generation to which he belonged. It was also to result in the
discovery of his own conscience.

I *Maternal Brittany*

Renan's natural birth occurred on February 28, 1823, but not
until twenty-two years had passed did he emerge from the supernatural womb of Catholicism.

The first phase of his life is taken up almost entirely by his
growing awareness that his conscience would not allow him to
continue professing the Catholic faith into which he had been
born. This long struggle with his belief assumed all the more
dramatic form, since he was not only a believer but also a candidate for the priesthood. The scene of his struggle was the seminary itself; its dénouement was achieved in October, 1845, when,
on the threshold of receiving the first "major order" (the *sous-
diaconat*), which commits its recipient irrevocably to the priesthood, he withdrew from the great Saint-Sulpice seminary in
Paris, leaving the ecclesiastical world behind him for the secular
world of learning and reason.

Readers at all familiar with Renan know his version of this
religious crisis as presented in what is, after *Vie de Jésus*, perhaps his second most famous book, *Souvenirs d'enfance et de
jeunesse* (1883). My reason for choosing not to turn immediately to this precious autobiographical source has nothing to do
with any fetish of chronological order or with any distrust of
the filter of memory, which long ago proved its worth as an instrument of artistic creation. The story of the young Renan of
fifteen to twenty-three as told by the Renan of sixty has its own
profound meaning, its own kind of truth, which I shall discuss in
a later chapter.

Fortunately we need not rely on Renan's retrospect alone, for
we possess more than one hundred letters which, from the three
Parisian seminaries in which he was trained (Saint-Nicolas du
Chardonnet, Issy, and Saint-Sulpice), he wrote to his mother, his
sister Henriette, his brother Alain, and to two friends, seminarians
in Brittany, Guyomard and Liart, between 1838 and 1846. We
also possess his *Cahiers de jeunesse*, or youthful notebooks, of
1845-1846. Although neither letters nor notebooks belong to

"literature" in the same sense as the letters of Madame de Sévigné or Flaubert or the journals of Baudelaire or Gide (works that have become a consecrated part of the French literary tradition), they are essential to the probing of Renan's mind in its formative stages and constitute a natural gateway to what will be, more strictly speaking, his literary work. Yet we are concerned here with more than mere documentary records of his struggle; they are writings also of uniquely dramatic literary qualities that spring in great part from their very lack of polish and from their complete naturalness.[1]

The earliest associations of Renan's childhood, many of which are referred to in his *lettres de famille* and others of which must be sought in his mature works, provide the materials for a broad sketch of his first "world." His innermost being was shaped by his Breton heritage, which also becomes one of his major themes. Brittany—by which we must be careful to specify the Armorican Peninsula, the *Bretagne bretonnante* where Breton is spoken— meant many things to Renan. It meant to some extent a physical landscape, "a cold wind, full of uncertainty (*vague*) and sadness, rising and carrying the soul toward other thoughts; treetops stripped of their leaves and writhing; the heath (*la bruyère*) prolonging afar its uniform color; the granite rock piercing through a soil too thin to give it covering; a sea almost always somber and forming on the horizon its circle of eternal groanings." But above all, this ancient and mysterious province, and the other Celtic lands to which it is akin, signified to Renan a spiritual landscape, and one by no means of such somber coloring: "a timid, reserved race, living entirely from an inner life, heavy in appearance, but capable of deep feeling and characterized in its religious instincts by an exquisite refinement (*une adorable délicatesse*)."[2]

A closer look at the family into which Renan was born gives us further reason not to depict his first world as especially somber. It is true that his father, a merchant-mariner, drowned under mysterious circumstances when Ernest was still a child (a loss to which he almost never refers); it is also true that the frail boy himself almost failed to survive childhood illness.[3] But from the beginning he was surrounded by the strongest affection of family and friends. His early letters dwell frequently on this affection; he calls it a plant that grows only in Brittany, and signs one of his letters *avec une sincère et bretonne affection*. He felt intense loyalty to his *petit pays*, Tréguier and surroundings, at one point wondering whether someone from fifteen miles away

could be called a true Breton, and at another, finding a fellow
seminarian likeable, "even though from Burgundy."

Few French writers have been blessed with the tender mother-
son relationship that Renan enjoyed; it was completely free of
the troubled overtones of a Baudelaire or a Proust. From this *très
chère maman*, this *bien bonne mère*, he inherited his own goodness (*bonté*) and mildness (*douceur*). He acknowledges these
qualities in himself, but without offensive pride, almost as though
they were biological gifts for which he could take no credit.
To his mother also he owed, certainly, his good humor (*ma mère,
à qui je dois le fond de ma nature, qui est la gaieté*), and perhaps, though some genealogists have found his explanation here
to be far-fetched, that gently mocking laughter which he claimed
came to him by way of her Gascon origins. Although young
Renan knew suffering, a major cause of which was precisely
separation from his mother, aggravated later by the thought of
frustrating her wish to see him become a priest, he remained a
stranger to those darker afflictions conveyed by the French words
ennui and *chagrin*. (The letters make this suffering clear, in contrast to the autobiography, which plays it down.) His character,
differing sharply in this respect from Flaubert's or Baudelaire's,
he describes as "not naturally inclined to melancholy"; for his
happy ignorance of the taste of that particular "weed" (*mauvaise
herbe*) he had above all his mother to thank.

The "delightful trio" (*le délicieux trio*) is completed by the
remarkable Henriette, whom he will later ennoble, like a heroine
of classical (i.e., Cornelian) tragedy or of a funeral oration by
Bossuet, in *Ma sœur Henriette*. The letters reveal her, without
need of fictional embellishment, as heroic enough. In his rela-
tions with her, prior to his marriage, we *do* find something of the
repressed or sublimated erotic feeling of the sexually immature
son for his mother. She was indeed his "second mother," but she
was also his only true confidante, and, since he believed friendship strongest when based on blood ties, his truest friend. Unlike widow Renan, whose dream was to give her son to the
Church, Henriette, having preceded Ernest into unbelief (and a
somewhat aggressively anti-clerical unbelief, at that), stood in
horror of seeing the inexperienced adolescent commit himself to
a vocation that might prove later to be false.

Renan was no passive object in her hands, as some critics have
claimed. His energy and will-power (*volonté*) became, if they
were not from the outset, as strong as hers. But without her
counsel, it is doubtful that he would have succeeded, in quite

the way he did, in "courageously shaking off a destiny which had imposed itself upon him most fatally" (his words to her), or in "making his own fate" (her words to him: *se faire un sort est une chose bien difficile*). This maiden sister, whose harsh existence did little to relieve her disposition to melancholy and whose only joys were his, was the chief instrument in securing Renan's passage from the clerical to the secular world. She remains one of the noblest *sœurs d'écrivain* in French literary history, her memory indissolubly bound to that of her great brother.

At the source of Renan's experience, thus, lies a generally blissful world, less exotic and haunting than Leconte de Lisle's native Ile Bourbon (*l'île édenique*) or than Baudelaire's *innocents paradis*, but comparable to these in potentiality for poetry, as well as in the strength and consolation they gave to his life. The sea may indeed have "groaned eternally" only a short distance away, but almost everything else—the quiet hours of study, the happy conversations and walks with mother and friends, the cocoon-like web of affection and solicitude that sheltered him—composed a peaceful image.

All the more terrible, then, the separation from this paradise for the adolescent wrenched from it and plunged into the "immense abyss" (*immense gouffre*) of Paris. His letters return again and again to the motifs of homesickness and the memory of a happier world. References to the painful separation recur like a lamentable refrain on almost every page (*Qu'il est pénible d'être séparés!*). I insist on this motif because I do not believe that it has been given proper weight in the explanation of Renan's religious crisis. I am convinced that this uprooting, or what the French call in a word heavy with moral connotations, *dépaysement,* is as important a cause of his loss of faith as the purely intellectual arguments upon which he himself, retrospectively, and most interpreters after him, have laid such stress. Exile was as much responsible as philosophical skepticism for undermining his childhood religion. His letters are those of an exile, or, more precisely, when we join to them his mother's and sister's replies, a network of letters (almost a novel in letter form, a *roman par lettres*) by three loved-ones exiled from one another: Madame Renan in Brittany, Ernest in Paris (his loneliness alleviated by summer vacation visits to Tréguier), Henriette, most sadly of all, in Poland as governess in an aristocratic family. As Renan gained more confidence in his intellect and in his power to shape his own life, the "Parisian abyss" becomes an essential theater of his development, which he had no desire to leave by returning permanently to Brittany ("I cling to Paris as to my life, *Je tiens à Paris comme à ma vie*"). His aim then becomes to reunite the "delightful trio" in Paris. His letters constantly look back to the happy union, seek to preserve it by the very fidelity and fervor with which they are written, and work toward reunion as part of the labor of restoring an equilibrium that has been disturbed.

II   *Piety and Talent: Saint-Nicolas du Chardonnet*

Renan owed his first moral education to these two women; he owed the rest of it to priests. In focusing more sharply on the clerical nature of his early world, one notes first that he seems almost to have been born into the clergy. Tréguier itself, the birthplace of Saint Yves, the most famous of Breton saints, was an "ecclesiastical town" where cloister shaded off into world almost imperceptibly, the devoutly religious center of a devoutly religious, though notoriously heterodox, province.[4] His feeling that he was somehow predestined to the priesthood was confirmed when his mother revealed to him—he was in Issy and twenty years old at the time—a long kept secret: she had, out of gratitude to Our Lady of Good Help (*Notre Dame de Bon Secours*), to whom she believed they owed his survival as a child, vowed that she would never place any obstacle in the way of his entering the Good Lord's service. The moral formation given him by his mother at home led smoothly into the education given him by the priests of the Collège de Tréguier, so many surrogate fathers for him, or small replicas of God the Father, whom he believed to be guiding his course with loving care—that is, until he began to suspect that the same God might be misleading him.

Renan never denied either the excellent scholastic or the excellent moral training lavished upon him by the priests of Tréguier. Fructifying the "peaceful and studious tastes" (*les goûts paisibles et studieux*) his mother had already implanted, this training seemed in turn to point naturally and without question to the seminary; all the more so, since, for this bright but relatively poor boy, the seminary was the only path open to a higher education. This last fact is extremely important. It means that from the beginning the danger to Renan's vocation (if one views his vocation as the desired goal) was present in the possibility that the end—the vocation—would become merely a means to something more important for him, the pursuit of knowledge as an end in itself.

The basic structure of the seminary training received by Renan had been fixed in the seventeenth century, and remained unchanged, essentially, in his time as it remains unchanged in ours. By way of "rhetoric" in the minor or junior seminary, the candidate is prepared for the two phases of the major seminary, first, philosophy, and then, as the crowning discipline (philosophy is merely its handmaid), theology.

At Saint-Nicolas du Chardonnet Renan first learned what it meant to write well and to take pride in writing well. But here also he learned to distinguish between writing well according to the traditional formulas of *la rhétorique,* whose grotesque contortions he rejected with some violence as unbecoming to a serious mind, and something quite different: *la littérature.* This, he promises, "will always delight me" (*fera toujours mes délices*). He took well to the simple, peaceful routine of Saint-Nicolas, with its gently paternalistic priests led by the refined Mgr. Dupanloup, later to become one of the most famous nineteenth-century French bishops. But the first shadows begin to fall. A "change in his spirit" begins with the departure of Henriette for Poland, leaving a "void" in his life. He complains of the difficulty of being transplanted when one is Breton, and speaks of his "exile." However, one must be careful not to exaggerate these shadows. The word *scepticisme* occurs for the first time under Renan's pen, but in a light-hearted context, as an amusing word, like *stoïque,* to be bandied about with his classmates. An atmosphere of piety envelops this great child of eighteen; his saddest thought is that he cannot lay his head more often on his mother's breast; he is still very much the believer.

III *Doubtful Philosophy: Issy*

As initiates into the study of philosophy, the seminarians at Issy are no longer treated as children. At first Renan finds the greater distance maintained by the priests between themselves and their charges, the greater freedom accorded by masters to pupils, disconcerting. But he loses little time in responding to the confidence placed in him. He begins to assert his independence. Late in 1841 we note the first little signs of a diminishing zeal for his spiritual vocation. He complains of the excessive length of the pious exercises and reveals how he finds painful (*pénible*), and how he resists, being "forced to the good" (*forcé au bien*). By May, 1842, he confesses to Liart that he is "too poor in piety" (*trop pauvre de piété*), and asks his friend's prayers that he may persevere in the vocation to which God "seems"—the verb is most revealing—to have called him.

Spiritual dryness such as this is not unusual in the devout, even in mystics. It need not be fatal. But in Renan's case it is accompanied by—perhaps, more accurately, caused by—growing intellectual difficulties. The upshot of his encounter with philosophy is to discover how difficult, if not impossible, it is to establish certainty (*certitude*) in any matter, especially the kind of historical certainty essential to proving the truth of the Catholic religion. Long before the first references in his letters to the study of Hebrew and to historical criticism of the Bible, and early in his struggles with the demon of philosophy, it is this general problem of establishing the *certain* truth of any proposition which gnaws at the entrails of his faith. *Difficultés*, he writes (the very word occurs now with increasing frequency, as does the word *sceptique*), are to found everywhere, and where he least suspected them. To Liart he denies being a skeptic, but he also admits finding the arguments designed to refute the skepticism of Pascal, Descartes, and Kant less impressive than the alleged "errors" of these philosophers. Yet he longs for certainty and turns with relief to the only discipline where he finds "necessary and absolute truth" (*le vrai nécessaire et absolu*), namely, mathematics. The certainty of mathematics compensates him for the lack of certainty in philosophy—at least for a time. All this is not too hopeful: few believers, and hardly any priests, are made by mathematical proofs; the age-old claim of Catholic orthodoxy still remains that faith, while surpassing reason, must not contradict reason.

If Renan at this point resists the temptation to "embrace a universal skepticism" (letter of September 1842 to Henriette), it is not because of mathematics but because he is still moved by his reading of the Bible and because he is sustained by the examples of Pascal and Kant, "the father of modern skeptics." If Pascal found no inconsistency between skepticism and the Catholic faith, or Kant no inconsistency between skepticism and idealistic beliefs akin to cherished religious doctrines, why should *he*? Later, the example of Malebranche, a bold disciple of Descartes, yet a priest, will re-enforce these other examples and persuade him, momentarily, that there is room in Catholic orthodoxy, even in the priesthood, for skeptics.

Curiously, in view of all this, one searches in vain in these letters for a precisely developed or very concrete discussion, with
Henriette or Liart, of any particular philosophical argument pos-
ing an obstacle to belief. Intellectual difficulties are important,
but referred to almost invariably in the most general terms.
Have they perhaps been exaggerated as a cause of Renan's
unbelief? On the other hand, in the dialectical exchange with
Henriette, beginning late in 1842, another type of argument is
introduced, to be insisted upon with increasing intensity: this is
the moral argument of choosing one's own fate, of "shaking off
a destiny imposed upon oneself" by others. This motif is summed
up in the recurrent words *décision* and *démarche* (a step to be
taken). The full force of the agonizing dilemma is conveyed in
the terrible phrase, *démarche décisive et irrévocable*.

I do not wish to go so far as to claim that philosophical arguments carried no real weight for Renan. The texts themselves
belie such an interpretation. Philosophical and moral objections
blend inseparably into each other, re-enforce each other subtly,
in his mind. I merely suggest that Renan's break from seminary
as well as from Church was more a matter of asserting his moral
freedom than of satisfying the demands of pure reason. At least
the hypothesis is not so absurd as it sounds. Nor would it remove
one iota of dignity from his struggle to achieve his authentic
nature.

With a dramatic effect in no way invented or contrived, but
springing from the very conditions they describe so spontaneously, these *lettres du séminaire* carry the reader along through
succeeding crises and peripeteias to the final resolution. As Renan
approached the minor order of the tonsure, which normally
closes the year of philosophy, he became less and less content
to "follow the impulsions given to him by others" (*suivre les
impulsions que l'on me donnait*), more and more determined to
examine his own will attentively, to know it, to act according to
it. In one of his most agitated letters, that of June 6, 1843, explaining to his mother his decision to delay the tonsure, he mentions for the first time a new voice rivalling that of duty to her
or to his directors: the voice of his own conscience. It commands
him imperiously, but not at once, to abandon all hope of the
priesthood. To Henriette's clear-cut urgings that he satisfy his
need for a quiet studious life by becoming a lay professor, to her
blunt warnings that a priest can never be a "free agent," he
opposes his compromise solution: to eschew the parish ministry
for which he is obviously unqualified, to be a scholarly priest

keeping his unorthodox thoughts to himself (again Pascal comes
to his aid, with his *pensée de derrière la tête*), asserting an inner
freedom though he be outwardly subordinate to authority. He
is walking a tight-rope between mother's and sister's wishes.
But he is also defining and affirming his own will, in that polite
manner he had of being true to himself while appearing not to
contradict others.

IV *Theology and Major Crisis: Saint-Sulpice*

In October, 1843, Renan entered Saint-Sulpice and began the
study of theology. His nostalgia for Brittany is still strong, all
the more because of what he considers the "coldness" of this
institution; he compares it to a machine, running itself entirely
on "forms" and "rules," indifferent to the development of one's
individualité personnelle (the remark is profoundly revealing).
The terrible word *décision* returns to haunt him. Here, in this
almost traumatic experience of the young seminarian tormented
by the necessity of taking an irrevocable decision, may be the
source of the immense value that the mature Renan will place
on freedom of decision, and even more, on freedom of indecision.
The crux of his problem was this: how can we accept an authority or commit ourselves to a cause or a party which we may
eventually come to doubt? The painful uncertainties and struggles (*les pénibles incertitudes et douloureux combats*) into which
this dilemma plunged him contrast ironically with the earlier
combats of rhetoric which he had related in mock-epic style, as
if to show their essential meaninglessness, in happier days at
Saint-Nicolas. The contrast, furthermore, enables us to measure
the great moral and intellectual distance he has covered in less
than five years! Yet in January, 1844, he has enough belief to
accept the tonsure, and even enough piety to believe that his
doubts and struggles have been God's way of testing his vocation. He announces the good news to his mother in a letter
touchingly signed *E. R., clerc tonsuré*.

Calm returns to his embattled spirit with the tonsure, but the
calm is only momentary. In terms of the theater, the reader
senses at this point in his correspondence a false dénouement,
the passing illusion of a "happy ending," and knows that the final
act is about to begin. The signs have been accumulating in all
too great number and with all too great clarity that Renan's
struggle will not culminate in ordination to the priesthood. A
would-be priest who insists so repeatedly on the fact that none

of the orders he has received, or is about to receive, commits him irrevocably, hardly has the fervor, let alone the joyful anticipation, of a true vocation.

Theology he finds, significantly, a "somewhat dry" study, its defense of dogmas vitiated by a fatal weakness—dependence on outmoded medieval scholasticism. By contrast, he has begun, with a zeal that will never abate, the study of Hebrew. Although there is not a single reference in his letters yet (nor will there be) to the type of argument, drawn from Biblical exegesis, to which he will attach such weight in the autobiographical account of his religious crisis, it is already clear that this solid and precise linguistic discipline will provide him with the key needed to that historical understanding of Christianity which will, in his mind, supplant dogmatic Christian faith. Most striking of all, in the letters of 1844-1845, is the reader's realization that the idea of the priesthood has become for Renan a means to a quiet, relatively unselfish life of study, rather than an end in itself, a kind of symbolic state awaiting only an act of courageous lucidity on his part to be abandoned forever as a false dream.

The final break with Saint-Sulpice came in October, 1845. But the climax occurred much earlier, in the spring of the same year. Renan clung to his vocation by a thin thread, as the year began, hoping to be ordained and then to teach Hebrew in a new faculty set up by the Archbishop of Paris, where he felt he would be less restricted than in a religious order. But his inner revolt had gained such momentum by then that it was bound soon, by inexorable logic, to demand expression in his outward condition. In practical terms, this meant a new crisis of decision: the *sous-diaconat*. No longer can he tolerate a "semblance of freedom" (*une ombre de liberté*). His avowed goal now, a goal utterly incompatible with the true priestly spirit (though he does not yet seem to realize this), is the free pursuit of his own intellectual progress. In perhaps the most disconsolate pages of his whole correspondence (*désolantes pensées*, he calls these), in thoughts that come close, in this man incapable of bitterness, to being an outburst of bitterness, he perceives the danger of being trapped in a net (*un filet*), a web (*un réseau*), woven around him by superior forces. Promethean-like, though perhaps too gently and undefiantly for a true Prometheus, he will "break the bonds" (*briser les liens*) that tie him.[5] For the first time (March, 1845) he broaches to Liart, already a priest, a theme that appears often in his early writings: the abandonment of Jesus in

order better to follow Jesus. We can only surmise the shock with
which his friend received this monstrous paradox.

The confession we have awaited finally comes, in the truly
climactic letter of this intensely dramatic series (April 11, 1845,
to Henriette): "I do not believe enough," *Je ne crois pas assez*.
The hoped-for illumination from God dissolving his doubts has
not occurred; what has come in its place, the result of an "immense labor" pursued by his thought, is the discovery that Christianity, while proved by "rational verification" to be not wholly
false, is not absolutely true. Renan's reason is finally awake, and
the possibility of further compromise for him with orthodoxy is
finally destroyed.[6] A new motif appears: the resolve to take his
university diplomas (*prendre ses grades*) and to build his career
as a lay scholar. The word *démarche* has lost its painful uncertainty and is now filled with hope. From Poland, Henriette, a
Cassandra who had foreseen his "cruel uncertainties," now exults
in the strength of his will (his *force de volonté*), in his *énergie*
and *résolution*—qualities without which, she adds, one must
remain all one's life only *un grand enfant*.

V *The Secular Arena*

Once Renan had decided, in July, 1845, to withdraw from
Saint-Sulpice as soon as possible, his only remaining problem was
how to make a place in the "larger theater" of secular life. It is
Renan himself who states, with pained perplexity, the theme of
the "two worlds" which I have chosen as title of this chapter
(letter to Henriette, July 21, 1845). "And this whole world [the
clerical] in which I have become naturalized, and which will now
deny me! . . . And will the other world have anything to do
with me? The first loved and pampered me; how much does it
not still have to say to me? Henriette, my good Henriette, sus-
tain my courage." His nostalgia for the earlier world of faith,
for simple and childlike belief, a nostalgia he will continue to
feel for several years afterward, is most intense at this turning
point of his career.

Yet the fact is that the transition between the "two worlds"
had already begun long ago, and in many curious ways. When
Renan the autobiographer declares, "So I descended, never to
mount them again in cassock, the steps of Saint-Sulpice, October
6, 1845," he is, quite pardonably, exaggerating for dramatic
effect. Actually the sorties from seminary had been numerous,
the invasions of "outside world" into seminary, numerous also,

almost from the beginning. There is no denying the world of
vétusté (ancientness) in which Renan had been soaked, from
Tréguier onward: the Breton piety, the Catholic dogmas unchanged for centuries, the priests whose habits (in both senses)
bespoke the seventeenth century. But between this world and the
modern world a subtle interpenetration was at work for Renan
in many ways, both large and small. The *charmante promenade,*
the delightful spectacle, to which Renan was much later to
compare his whole progress across the nineteenth century—the
image shocked many of his readers as frivolous—is already contained in germ in the many lesser *promenades* and *spectacles*
he describes, as a seminarian, with such relish to his mother:
the French landscape as seen from stagecoach between Paris
and Brittany, the many excursions granted the seminarians, to
Versailles, to Chantilly, into the heart of Paris. He is not so
turned in upon his intellectual struggle that he cannot find time
to enjoy the magnificent view of Paris from Issy; and after all,
that arch-symbol of modernity, the railroad, skirted the ancient
parks and arbors of Issy where he walked in the footsteps of
Bossuet and Fénelon, who, two hundred years before on this
very site, had argued questions of theology.

News of "modern," that is, Romantic, literature had already
reached the students of rhetoric at Saint-Nicolas. Hugo and
Lamartine were discussed there eagerly, so many cracks in the
prison wall of a closed religious system (to turn against Claudel,
somewhat maliciously, a famous phrase of his).[7] Most exciting
of all for Renan, the future historian, had been the discovery of
the Romantic historian Michelet. "I learned with astonishment,"
he wrote in his *Souvenirs,* "that there were serious and learned
laymen; I saw that something existed outside of antiquity and
the Church, and in particular that there was a contemporary
literature worthy of attention. The death of Louis XIV no longer
marked the end of the world for me. Ideas and feelings appeared
to me which had found expression neither in antiquity nor in
the seventeenth century."

Still another kind of contact with the layman's world had been
frequent for Renan long before he descended those steps of
Saint-Sulpice so definitively. Some of his fellow seminarians at
Issy and Saint-Sulpice were much older men, whose vocation
had bloomed late in life. Coming from all professions, they
formed what Renan calls a "Noah's ark" in the midst of the
Parisian world. While one resembled a "seventeenth-century mag-
istrate," another, more disturbingly, had been a *professeur d'*

histoire, whose experience did nothing to remove Renan's doubts
about being able to find certainty in the study of history, let
alone in the so-called "historical proofs" of the Catholic faith.
Finally, not only did Renan himself receive permission, while
still a seminarian, to attend courses in Hebrew at the Sorbonne
and the Collège de France, but two of his clerical teachers had
themselves been formed at the University of Paris: Abbé Pinault,
a physicist, whose digressions on the history and the "proper
spirit" of science were received "with the greatest interest" by
the future author of *L'Avenir de la science;* and his fellow Breton
and professor of Hebrew, Abbé Le Hir. This extraordinary man,
though he disappointed Renan's hopes that he would provide
orthodoxy's answer to rationalist German exegesis, first inspired
in him the vocation of the Hebraist.

Gradual and smooth though Renan's passage from seminary
to world may thus have been (he himself was determined to
avoid *brusque sécularisation,* to effect the transition in a manner,
above all, painless for his mother), he was still engaged in
struggle. But the nature of the struggle differed markedly now
from the wrestling with fate and with conscience that had pre-
occupied him earlier. There is naturally a corresponding difference in tone between the letters dating, roughly, from before
October, 1845, and those dating after. The content of these letters from the Collège Stanislas and the Pension Crouzet, semi-
ecclesiastical halfway houses where Renan eked out his living
as a tutor while preparing his titles to a more remunerative post,
is no less absorbing for the reader who has followed him this
far than the content of earlier letters. But what fascinates us
now are qualities of intelligence and shrewdness, of extraordinary industry and ambition. The drama has turned from an
intellectual into a professional one; the record of a mind strug-
gling for freedom merges into the timetable of a career being
constructed, this time, on lasting foundations. "I am not at all
behind schedule," he remarks at one point. "Nothing can stop
me," he assures Henriette as his confidence in his ability flowers.
He becomes a kind of *force qui va,* to borrow Hugo's description
of his Romantic hero; but the resemblance is only superficial,
for he lacks the essential qualities of such a hero: fatalism and
the abandonment to instinct. Besides, he is inwardly very happy
and has a future.

In the space of two years (January, 1846–January, 1848), this
"son of peasants and poor sailors, covered with the triple ridicule of being a fugitive from the seminary, an unfrocked cleric,

and a hard-shelled pedant," as he calls himself in the *Souvenirs,*
takes his *baccalauréat,* his *licence,* wins the distinguished Prix
Volney for his first learned work (an essay on Semitic languages), advances well into his doctoral theses, becomes a member of the Société Asiatique, and makes all the personal contacts
so necessary in France to the obtaining of a good position. In
fact, by February, 1847, he is ready to allude to the strong
possibility of his succession to the post he covets, the Chair of
Hebraic, Chaldean, and Syrian Languages at the Collège de
France. A thousand *ruses,* a thousand *précautions,* the constant
exercise of that very faculty Renan later claimed he lacked—
practical intelligence—went tirelessly into this carving out of
his academic niche. It is surely one of the most amazing feats
in the history of French scholarship. Once again, Henriette
reached out by letter, this time to see that the proper influence
(*tous ces hommes distingués*) worked in his favor; he was seldom alone. But friends and protectors would have meant nothing, in the field he had chosen, without his intrinsic merit.

The atmosphere of sustained, unremitting application of self
to an attainable goal pervading these post-seminary letters gives
them a certain dryness. Renan himself speaks of his *travaux
arides et continus* and compares the dryness (*sécheresse*) of
his present life to the "pure joys" of his childhood. Yet, there
is a kind of moral drama here, too. It arises from the spectacle
of an idealistic, timid, reserved young provincial discovering
with some horror the côteries that rule the academic world, but
determined to make himself known *sans intrigue et sans jactance*
(without boasting), without abasing himself, vanquishing with
patient good humor and pure talent a new monster, bureaucratic
red-tape (*administration paperassière*). There is drama also, of
an austerely beautiful kind, in the theme of the "two existences"
he must lead in this transitional phase. Not unlike the poor
novelist alone with his muse in a garret, Renan is the poor
scholar in his bare *pension* room (this, his *vie extérieure*), but
knowing the inner happiness—an "incredibly full happiness,"
une incroyable plénitude de bonheur—of scholarly thought and
a pure conscience. The equation is exactly reversed from Saint-
Sulpice, where his outward life was sheltered and comfortable,
his inner life tormented by doubts. The converging of three
wills, his now dominant, toward a happier domestic future, "our
future" (*notre avenir*), as Renan writes, provides an element of
suspense. Not for one moment does he lose sight of this long-
sought goal, as important to him as the goal of a distinguished

academic post: the reunion of mother, brother, and sister; the
termination of "this life of suffering and exile."

VI   *Une région assez calme*

The *lettres de famille,* which we have followed down to what
Renan calls "the first literary event of my life," the Prix Volney,
and to the threshold of his first major work, *L'Avenir de la
science,* foreshadow in several ways attitudes characteristic of
the mature writer. Renan knew suffering, however much he
would mute this theme in his later works. Yet, at the core of
his being is an unchanging serenity. Describing what he calls
souffrances intimes and *cruelles perplexités* to his sister, in one
of his most moving letters (April 11, 1845), he nevertheless
observes, with a touch of wonderment, "there still existed in the
depth of my being a region that is quite calm" (*il y avait au
fond de mon être une région assez calme*).[8] Even the smile (*le
sourire*) we associate especially with his relaxed, bemused old
age, the mocking smile that has mystified so many, is present
from the earliest of these letters, coexisting with intense seriousness. *Sourire* occasionally deepens into *rire,* laughter. They exercise themselves on the foolishness of rhetoric or on the foibles
of his professors; but once, at least, when he speaks of being
able to laugh at his own dreams, a broader, more philosophic
and ironic gaiety, like that of the mature Renan, breaks through.

Dependent on the affection of loved ones, as well as on intellectual stimulation from others—books, teachers, what he calls
causes excitatrices—he nevertheless needs only himself, his own
"center of happiness" (*centre de bonheur*), the enjoyment of his
own thoughts and feelings. *Jouissance,* enjoyment, is a key word
of the seminarian, strangely enough, long before it enters into
the master's ripe paradoxes. Egoism? Yes, perhaps, but only in
the same mysterious way that many great writers manage to
combine exaltation of self with profound interest in others.[9]
Political allusions are few and oblique in these early letters,
but even here there is prefiguring of the kind of action that
Renan will favor. He is both *contemplatif,* turned inward, and
alert observer of his political surroundings. A "well born soul"
(*une âme bien née,* no blood or social aristocracy here, but
something wholly spiritual), naturally refined and bearing his
privileged Breton heritage of *adorable délicatesse,* whatever revolt he manages against the order of things will never be gross
or coarse. One has only to listen to how he, along with Hen-

riette, uses the word *vulgaire* ("commonplace") to predict that whatever action he will take to change the world will not be outwardly rebellious or noisily iconoclastic, but basically conservative and of the kind that veils its boldness prudently.

Contradictory qualities? Certainly. "I contradict myself? very well, then, I contradict myself" (Walt Whitman). Dualities, if not dichotomies, are also part of the earliest Renan, particularly of his religious thought. God is, somehow, both Deceiver and Providence, and we are both blessed and misled, like so many "playthings of error." How could he have concluded otherwise, having been eased with unparalleled solicitude into a religious vocation and then deprived of a certainty that seemed fixed in the nature of things? God had deceived him (*Dieu m'a trahi*), leading him into an "inextricable net" while his reason slept. But from this error, at least, he escapes, when God as revealed truth becomes God as the voice of "reason" and "conscience." Renan already tends toward his extraordinary wager with Christianity: he will remove from it the supernatural while preserving most of its essential moral teachings.

Thus, when Renan reassures his mother that he remains "as she formed him" that "there will never be a break (*une scission*) between my past life and my life to come," and that his two lives "form a single whole, no instant of one being lost for the other," for once he is not "coloring" the facts to make them more palatable to her. He is simply stating a prophetic truth about the work he will create. Radical though the changes of outlook are which carry Renan from one world to another, one life to another, he is already determined upon what may be his greatest, as well as his most underrated, achievement: the arrangement of his dualities and contradictions into a coherent, unified, and tranquil whole.

CHAPTER 2

Joseph's Cistern

RENAN'S *lettres de famille* for the period I have surveyed, roughly a decade (1838-1848), serve less as a journal of ideas than as a journal of his general intellectual and moral progress, of the crises he weathers, the courses of action he resolves upon. For more direct knowledge of the "immense labor" pursued by his thought, the "vast inner controversy" (*la vaste controverse intérieure*), alluded to but not described in detail in his letters, we must turn to two other sources: the *Cahiers de jeunesse*, a series of nine notebooks composed in 1845-1846, and *L'Avenir de la science, pensées de 1848*.[1] The dominant theme of both these writings (one hesitates to call them "works" since the first is a private notebook and the second, though intended for publication, is more an attempt at a work, a vast *essai*, than a finished product) is Renan's striving to recompose an organically whole belief worthy to replace the Catholic synthesis he has rejected. There is something fragmentary about both writings, even the second, despite its great length; it is as though their author is reassembling pieces, some old, some new, into a system of ideas that he can call his own. He is also in search of his originality, both of thought and of form.

I *Obstacles to Self-Knowledge*

The Catholic critic, Charles Du Bos, in his own journal, considered Renan's *Cahiers* to be unparalleled in French literature for their frankness and sincerity.[2] To be sure, there is a certain innocent nudity about them. Renan himself compares the orthodox believer, safely encased in his shell (*carapace*) to *l'homme nu dans la simple beauté de ses formes*. He resembles that naked figure, though at this stage he is less in possession of his "forms," in either the philosophical or the literary sense, than in quest of them. But for all the frank attention he gives in the *Cahiers* to "myself" (*Moi-même* is the title, also provided in Hebrew, of the Fifth Notebook), a great secretiveness prevails about his

34

deeper or more poetic nature. The author himself calls our attention several times to the fact that his notebooks are not truly intimate.

The reasons for this absence of intimacy in what nevertheless remains, intellectually, a most revealing dialogue with self, are worth dwelling upon for a moment. To know oneself, first of all, as Renan acknowledges in a passage of *L'Avenir de la science* relevant to my analysis of his *Cahiers,* is immensely difficult. Many of us, he claims with perhaps more rhetoric than truth, have experienced moments of descent into ourselves, piercing layer after layer and reaching close to our true depths, "where conventions expire and we are face to face with ourselves without fiction or artifice" (*en face de soi-même sans fiction ni artifice*). However, such moments are rare and fleeting: "Habitually we live opposite a third person, who prevents the frightening contact of the ego with itself" (*une tierce personne, qui empêche l'effrayant contact du moi contre lui-même*). True frankness, he concludes, is attained only when we dare "pierce this intermediary veil" and listen to the unselfish instincts that incline us "to know, to adore, and to love" (*savoir, adorer, et aimer*). (It is curious, in passing, to compare what young Renan finds beneath the surface of conventional behavior with what a pessimist like La Rochefoucauld finds, namely, selfishness; the former may be overly optimistic about mankind, if not about himself.) A characteristic Renanian image appears here, that of the veil to be penetrated or lifted, whether the veil of self or the veil of supernatural religious mysteries. At this point in his life, the principal obstacle between the "I" and itself seems to lie in an over-developed critical sense, an exaggerated fear of being "duped," which would compel him to consider every inspiration as a mechanism to be dismantled, every instinct of beauty or truth as naive.

Another obstacle to self-knowledge is vanity, in Renan's case his tendency to hide imperfections ("I patch myself up," *Je me rafistole*), to think of appearances. Most disquieting of all is his tendency to say the opposite of what he means, in order to please others or to conform to their image of him. All this is very human, even attractively so. The special meaning of such remarks for the student of Renan is the striking way in which they foreshadow his latter-day disposition to create a myth of himself, part of whose success lay in being what an amused public wished him to be. As if these lions in the path of self-determination were not forbidding enough, he notes a further

problem. Reality and dream are so intertwined in our lives (a
reference to the well-known theme of Calderón) that we can
never separate them completely. To this limitation inherent in
our existence Renan seems resigned. The being that he was in
dreams and that eluded him plays some role, though a marginal one, in his *Cahiers*. From the Hebrew word he uses for
"thoughts," the precise meaning of which is "thoughts in dreams,
afterwards recalled," we are led to expect almost a kind of do-it-
yourself exercise in psychoanalytical exploration. But the stuff
of which his dreams are made is suggested only incidentally:
nostalgia for Brittany, for the purity of childhood friendships,
for his innocent faith in Jesus. This part of himself seems to
have been struck by blight (*tout cela flétri en moi*); the motifs
of dessication and withering are frequently touched upon. But
a fundamental reserve keeps him from probing further, at least
in these notebooks. They express, he explicitly tells us (or tells
himself, to be more accurate), only "the most superficial results"
of his thinking; they fail to divulge his "gentle, weak, and pensive childhood . . . the finest part of myself" (*douce, faible, et
pensive enfance, . . . la plus belle partie de moi-même*).

Only here and there, in rapid sketches of poetic projects—a
philosophical poem on the Knight of Ideas (*le chevalier des
idées*) who will finally reconcile Beauty, Truth, and Goodness,
or a "novel completely about the soul" (*un roman tout psychique*)—do the *Cahiers* point to the type of imaginative effort
at depicting an ideal self in which Renan will in fact engage in
the so-called *fragments romanesques* and in other more "intimate" works to be discussed in a later context.[3] The most elaborate and public of such images will be his *Souvenirs d'enfance
et de jeunesse*. To look ahead a moment, in such more imaginative self-portraits, what Renan has called *fiction* and *artifice*
will serve, not as ruses to obstruct true self-knowledge, but, in
their more positive, poetic senses, as devices for grasping and
describing his deeper nature.

But the author of the *Cahiers* is still far from mastering the
artistic power necessary to create what he will later call his
"poetry of the self."

II *Lines of Speculation*

Though lacking in the confessional quality of so many French
literary diaries, the *Cahiers de jeunesse* reveal, as few so-called
intimate journals do, the ferment of a young man's intellectual

life, in its unadorned and occasionally even crude state. A whole
inner universe, kept something of a secret in the seminary and
only partially disclosed in the correspondence, rises to the surface in these pages. They are (an example of the crudity) *vomi-
toires,* an emetic for his ideas, a funnel through which his matter
is discharged. According to the more dignified descriptions in
the Hebrew chapter headings (not really an affectation, since
Renan was plunged in the study of Hebrew at the time), the
Cahiers are: a harvest (*Moisson*); a compendium of ideas, "useful for many things" (*Utile à beaucoup de choses*—here the title
is given in Greek); a record of his struggles (*Nephtali, J'ai lutté
les luttes de Dieu*); a cistern (*La citerne de Joseph*);[4] above all,
an eager and zestful affirmation of his newly liberated ego (*Moi-
même; Ma Vie*).

The special virtue of the *Cahiers* is, in fact, their very impurity
of form. To a large extent *cahiers* in the scholastic sense ("copy-
books"), filled with notations on books read and courses taken,
they also abound in philosophical and historical speculations.
Poetic effusions are juxtaposed with sharp, precise observations,
both about himself and about his university professors. Intense
consciousness of self does not exclude awareness of and preparation to communicate with a larger public. The true scholar is
"of the public" (*du public*) and must address himself to "all
thinkers" everywhere; he is not an end in himself, but a kind
of artisan whose works must be put into circulation if his existence is to be justified. Renan's avowal that he takes pleasure
in describing his sufferings, his happy discovery that "one ceases
to suffer what one suffers by describing it" (*on cesse de souffrir
ce qu'on souffre en le décrivant*), reveal him, even more con-
clusively than the delight he predicted he would always take
in literature, at Saint-Nicolas du Chardonnet, as the born writer.
Like an athlete flexing his muscles in private before entering the
arena, Renan in his *Cahiers* is readying himself to defend his
ideas on a larger field ("I will react against all these men when
the time comes," he promises himself, in disgust with the narrow-
mindedness of certain rationalist critics of Christianity).

To summarize the thought contained—the very verb seems
inappropriate—in these notebooks is a challenge. Renan speaks
of the courage and faith he needed in order to "pursue my
speculative line" (*poursuivre ma ligne spéculative*). Taking a
hint from this phrase and adapting it slightly, I shall try to sum
up the main "lines of speculation" discernible in this often disorderly mass of notes. The Renan of the *Cahiers* is groping

toward two or three major ideas which will serve as guidelines
to his independent system of thought. To define these ideas more
sharply, he must first confront and assess some of the great assumptions—Romantic assumptions, for the most part—of his age.

III   Literature and Criticism

The first such confrontation is with the very notion of "literature." Renan will eventually accept literature, as he will accept
criticism and scholarship, but not before he has subjected them
to ruthless cross-examination. *Littérature* is frequently a pejora-
tive term in the *Cahiers*. At one point he even suggests doing
away with this word altogether. The reasons for his antipathy
to literature are several. Fresh from training in one of man's
sublimest vocations, he needed convincing that the polishing of
phrases was something more than foolish vanity. Furthermore,
he was espousing the view, derived from the German eighteenth
century (especially Herder) and adapted into French by Madame de Staël and by the Romantic philosopher Victor Cousin,
that literary works written by individual authors with sophisticated intent (*littérature réfléchie*) were by nature inferior to
"primitive," impersonal works composed anonymously or collectively when humanity was still young (*littérature spontanée*).
From this standpoint he was bound to feel that outside of the
Bible, the Hindu epics, Homer, the popular poetic traditions of
Brittany, and the like, the rest is *mere* literature. Part of his
problem was to decide whether literature in his own time was
hopelessly decadent or had possibilities of rebirth and renewal.
His *bête-noire* is seventeenth-century classicism, especially Boi-
leau and Racine, the worst example of an excess of "reflection,"
of imprisonment in the finite (this opposition of *fini* and *infini*
is a stock Romantic notion). Only one modern poet expresses
the infinite, and recaptures in an *âge réfléchi* something of an
âge spontané: Lamartine, the hero of the *Cahiers*.[5]

Much of this critique is inherited from Romanticism. Renan
confesses to having been born a Romantic (*né romantique*),
that is, with a need for "the soul, something that places me at
the edge of the unfathomable depth" (*l'âme, quelque chose qui
me mette au bord de l'abîme*). At the same time, his dissatis-
faction with "literature" points ahead and will link him, modestly
enough, with the Symbolist poets who queried profoundly the
nature of literature, especially to raise doubts about the very
materials it must use—words. Words, he remarks, are too sharp

to be suitable for poetry, unless they are used, in Lamartinian fashion, vaguely, as symbols. Repeatedly he voices his fear that thought of any kind, not merely poetic thought, risks being distorted by too great precision.[6] Reality resembles not pigeon-holes with lines of demarcation (*casiers à ligne de démarcation*), but a picture whose shadings are imperceptible (*un tableau aux nuances insensibles*). Literature, handicapped already by a certain falseness inherent in the very act of writing, must somehow overcome the obstacle of words and render this *tableau*. Yet, despite his reservations, Renan finds hope for the literature of his age. Modern literary "decadence," he points out, is not to be confused with that of Greco-Roman antiquity. Philosophy may revitalize literature as it could not do in any Silver Age. Literature may even become a *quasi-religion nationale*. Furthermore, the "reflective age" has brought with it what he considered his century's greatest creation, namely, criticism.

The term "criticism" (*critique*) as Renan uses it is magnificently spacious. His descriptions of it in the *Cahiers* will be expanded into one of the major themes of *L'Avenir de la science*, the defense of "universal criticism" (*critique universelle*), which he will call "the only essential trait one can assign to the delicate, elusive, indefinable thought of the nineteenth century." That the once-noble term, criticism, could have shriveled up in our own time to the point where it means merely *literary* criticism would have caused Renan to marvel. He is severe in his private judgments of two reigning literary critics of his day: Villemain and Sainte-Beuve. Their criticism is largely a game, a pretense, reflecting the vain *jeu*, the *feinte* of contemporary literature itself. No literary critic around him measures up to his ideal as does Lamartine in poetry.[7] Yet just as he retained hope that literature, once rescued from the *littérateurs*, might again express something of humanity's aspirations, he saw great potentiality for modern criticism in two advantages it enjoyed over ancient criticism: (1) it had freed itself from the "preceptive" bias that obliged it constantly to judge, rather than allowing it to interpret historically, in relation to time and to country (he justly recognized Sainte-Beuve's positive contribution here); (2) by conceiving of "the beautiful" (*le beau*) as infinite, it had rid itself of the classical fetish of narrow, rigid formal perfectionism. Renan had not discovered that God is relative merely to believe that beauty is absolute.

Renan's deepest concern in the *Cahiers* is to justify criticism in his own eyes, as a positive, creative faculty. Of its function as a preservative from error, a protection against being duped and ridiculed, he was well enough convinced. But how reconcile it with his love of truth and virtue, his wish to "belong to God and to the ideal"? How make it a part of a new *sublime* worthy to supplant his religious faith? His inner debate over this problem, the emotional implications of which are reserved for the *Fragments romanesques,* may be summed up by considering his manner of reacting to two concepts current in French thought of the 1830's and 1840's: synthesis (*synthèse*) and eclecticism (*éclectisme*).

IV   A Vital and Comprehensive Philosophy

Renan will be satisfied with nothing less than what he calls a *philosophie vitale et compréhensive,* for this alone will enable him to harmonize within himself the divergent skills and insights of scholar, critic, philosopher, and poet. The magic words in this context, occurring repeatedly in both the *Cahiers* and *L'Avenir de la science,* are *synthèse, harmonie, vie, plénitude, tout.* His ideal is "to grasp the whole from every point of view" (*embrasser le tout de tous les points de vue*). Though at times he may allude with some regret to the "drying up" of an earlier faith and emotion, the characteristic emphasis of the *Cahiers* is nevertheless on life, and on life abundant, awaiting only a philosophical (and later a literary) structure vast enough to contain it. It is poignant to hear the future historian, who will live vicariously through several centuries of Judaism and several generations of Christianity, exclaim that he has "courage and zeal enough for several lives" (*du cœur et du feu pour plusieurs vies*).

Behind this striving for synthesis is an idea so bold that we have difficulty conceiving of it today, though to an age that had discovered the existence of Humanity it was almost a matter of simple logic: the idea that the individual is a mirror or microcosm of the "human spirit" (*l'esprit humain*). Renan's identification of his personal evolution with the evolution of humanity was an even bolder variation on this theme; it will become one of the very cornerstones of his whole work. The fullness of life, the harmonizing of divergent faculties, to which he aspires are qualities already possessed by humanity in its historical evolution. Whereas Flaubert had declared, "Outside of form, no salvation," Renan's new orthodoxy is much more generous and all-inclusive: outside of the human spirit in all its manifestations, no salvation. "All is ours; there is only one human spirit" (*Tout est à nous; il n'y a qu'un esprit humain*).[8]

The Renan who wrote these words has already been transformed from an anachronism—a double one, at that, both Breton and seminarian—into very much a child of his age. The idea of the all-embracing synthesis is one of the dominant themes of nineteenth-century, above all, of Romantic art and thought. It took many forms, including the fusion of artistic genres in fresh combinations; the harmonizing of philosophical concepts; the blending of multiple types of inspiration or truth into new organic wholes. I mention a few examples close to Renan's *Cahiers* and *L'Avenir de la science* in date. Comte's *sociologie* was intended to provide a synthesis correcting the errors of the theological and metaphysical ages of thought and flowering into a rational religion of humanity; he had completed his greatest work, the *Cours de philosophie positive*, in 1842, three years before Renan began his *Cahiers*. In 1842 also, Balzac, who is with Hugo and Wagner the most ambitious artistic synthesizer of the century, in his *Avant-Propos* to the first edition of the *Comédie Humaine*, had outlined his theory of the novel as a fusion of history and poetry, science and mysticism, drama and epic. Wagner's first great music-drama, *Tannhäuser*, was performed initially in 1844. Some critics find in it a truer application of Hugo's theories of the drama as total form subsuming epic and lyric (*Préface de Cromwell*, 1827) than Hugo was able to achieve in his own theater.[9]

Renan's originality as a synthesizer lies in his ambition to achieve totality of vision *as a scholar*. His professed guides, in the *Cahiers*, are neither Comte, Balzac, Wagner, nor Hugo, whatever his affinities with them may be. They are: Lamartine, whose attempts to fuse poetry and philosophy have paled beside the robust syntheses of Balzac and Hugo (Renan admired especially his abortive epic poem, *Jocelyn*); the comprehensive Germanic minds of Leibnitz, Goethe, and Herder ("my royal thinker," *mon penseur-roi*), whose universality he had discovered as part of his introduction into the "temple" of German culture; the great pioneer of Sanskrit studies in France, Eugène Burnouf, the "philosopher-scholar" to whom he will dedicate *L'Avenir de la science* and whom he frequently opposes to another of his professors, Etienne Quatremère, the model of pedantry to be avoided; and finally, Victor Cousin. To this once-famous thinker, Renan probably owes most of his terminology and ideas concerning synthesis.[10]

V *Three Ages and Two Ways of Judging*

Cousin, whose influence on nineteenth-century French philosophical and literary thought seems to have been much greater
than his real merits as a philosopher, is referred or alluded to
often in the *Cahiers,* as well as in *L'Avenir de la science.* At the
very time when Renan risked being intellectually drawn and
quartered by the opposing tendencies of his mind, and long
before he had learned how to let them all have their say within
the artistic framework of philosophical dialogue or drama, Cousin
made to his thought two important contributions which helped
him reconcile his contradictions: the historical concept of humanity's "three ages," and the philosophical method, also strongly
dependent on the historical approach, known as *eclecticism.*

Simplified, the theory of the "three ages" viewed humanity as
having begun its history with an instinctive and highly poetic
union of itself with the world outside it (the syncretic age),
as then having traversed the phase of separating itself from that
world (analytical or reflective age), and, finally, as achieving
true wisdom in a supreme form of rationalism integrating reason
with religion (the synthetic age). The analogy with Renan's
own progress was inescapable; and he did not fail to draw it.
His own childhood had been like the childhood of the human
spirit in its spontaneous, instinctive, and naive religious belief;
his awakening to reason corresponded to *l'âge analytique* or
réfléchi; he now stood, like humanity, on the threshold of the
age of synthesis.

I have already referred to the boldness of this concept. Yet
boldness and pride alternate curiously in the *Cahiers* with self-
doubts and anxieties. Renan seldom questioned, as a modern
reader might, whether "humanity" was anything more than an
abstraction, though he does at times question the central and
absolute place conferred upon it in the universe (by Hegel, for
example), or its "deificability." His reservations about Cousin's
doctrine relate primarily to the validity of the eclectic method.
Eclecticism, from the Greek "to pick out, to select," was basically a historically oriented philosophy which taught that no
one system can be wholly true or wholly false and that therefore only a method incorporating into its total view of things
the valid ideas of each system can lead us to the truth. Renan
perceived the grave logical difficulties that such a philosophy
raises. According to what touchstone are we to determine which
ideas in a given system are true and which are false? In the

light of what higher criterion are we to *choose?* He brought
other objections to bear upon eclecticism: is not to select ideas
in this fashion to "blunt" (*émousser*) the instrument of one's own
thought, to dull the edges of one's originality, or, as he calls it,
one's *physionomie?* How, furthermore, can we hope that our
composite system will survive the test of critical analysis, when
so many systems of the past have not? Although eclecticism
clearly appealed to him as a means of adjusting from belief in
absolute truth to belief in the relativity of truth, the fear still
lurked in his mind that thorough-going relativism may lead to
nihilism. The prospect, for example, of giving up entirely such
"absolutes" as the existence of the spiritual soul or the correspondence of virtue to a higher spiritual reality outside man is
disquieting to him.

How does the author of the *Cahiers* resolve this problem?
"Two ways of judging," he decides, "absolutely, eclectically;
I take now one, now the other, and would have difficulty in re-
stricting myself to one." This type of compromise, in which two
contradictory terms, *les deux faces de la vérité*, are allowed to
subsist, in which neither is excluded, already bears the stamp
of the mature Renan—except that with experience his need to
"judge absolutely" will grow less and less compelling. For the
moment, as he approaches *L'Avenir de la science*, the need is
still strong. There are two voices in the *Cahiers:* Renan the
dogmatist, proposing his beliefs with certitude and authority,
and Renan the critic, qualifying and doubting. That these two
voices carry over into *L'Avenir de la science* is apparent from
the rather startling term he chooses to define his method in this
next book: he is the "critical dogmatist" (*critique dogmatique*).

CHAPTER 3

Science as the New Religion

IN French literature, *L'Avenir de la science* is unique not only for the manner in which it saw the light: a manuscript published (1890) almost forty years after its composition (1848-1849), intact and virtually unrevised.[1] It is also unique in kind. Where else can we find a work that begins with a simple sentence of five words, "One thing alone is necessary!" (*Une seule chose est nécessaire!*), and then takes five hundred pages of printed text to tell us what the "one thing" is? Where else is there a work on the subject of man's most impersonal achievement, yet so personal as to take for its epigraph: "Flesh of my flesh and bone of my bone" (*Hunc nunc os ex ossibus meis et caro de carne mea*)? How many tributes to science are there that begin with a precept of Christ and end with a prayer?

I An Un-Cartesian Discourse on Method

Renan claimed, in a letter to Henriette of January, 1849, that this was his *Discours de la méthode*. But apart from the facts that both his and Descartes' works do deal with methodology, lay the foundations of a philosophy, and outline, often in prophetic manner, programs for a whole intellectual lifetime, they bear little resemblance to each other. Descartes is calm and rational where Renan is excessive and sometimes highly emotional in both thought and style. Descartes is indifferent to, when not rejecting outright, the study of history, the very cornerstone without which Renan's whole work would collapse. Despite his long Latinized constructions, Descartes makes clear, orderly, graceful reading, while Renan's thoughts are formless and his style, with its cumbersome repetitiveness, might repel readers from "science" rather than attracting them to it—sacrilegious though this may sound to those who know and admire only the mature stylist. Yet, as we shall see, it is a style perfectly suited to the theme, one reason certainly that the mature stylist saw fit not to revise his manuscript in any significant manner.

The only thing "analytical" about Renan's work is the *Table analytique*, a detailed summary of the contents, without which one would be truly lost in the overgrowth. No *tabula rasa* here, but a festive table groaning under the weight of sources and authorities. The massive text overflows into almost thirty pages of notes which are often exactly what notes should not be, that is, undigested bits of text. In this mosaic of sources, for which references are not always provided, it is difficult to tell what is Renan's thought and what is someone else's (a resemblance rather with Montaigne than with Descartes). This last may be, in Renan's case, a trait of youth, providing another contrast with Descartes, forty when he published his *Discours* and intent on defining what was his with the utmost purity. Renan's triumph will be to assert his strong personal identity *despite his sources*. Continuing something of the same "copybook" atmosphere, *L'Avenir de la science* is nevertheless quite different in form from the *Cahiers de jeunesse*. The latter is fragmentary, elliptical, and allusive; the former, essentially an essay expanded to indecorous length (developing in fact many of the themes of the *Cahiers*), and, since it is a public rather than a private work, distinctly more rhetorical in tricks of style. It is Renan's *Génie de la science*. Like that other great disorderly book, Chateaubriand's *Génie du christianisme*, with which I think it has a much closer kinship than with the *Discours de la méthode*, it is a work more famous than read, and known mostly through anthologized pages.

This may be an injustice. When read in long stages, allowing several months, *L'Avenir de la science* reveals, despite its extensiveness, a surprising quality of intensity. What gives it this intensity is Renan's absolute devotion to the "scientific" life as he understood it. Never in these interminable pages do we really lose sight of that "single necessary thing" of the initial sentence. The theme is first placed before us in the moving dedicatory letter to Burnouf, the master scholar who had confirmed, on the plane of purely lay values, the ideal of life already learned by Renan from his clerical teachers, the ideal of life conceived not as a role to play or as a matter of *intrigue*, but as a "true and serious thing" (*une chose sérieuse et vraie*). Briefly summarized in Renan's own words, the dominant theme is this: "science becoming philosophy, and obtaining the highest results from the most scrupulous analysis of details."

The component parts into which this major theme breaks down do not admit of easy summary. Not only do they touch on most of mankind's principal activities and disciplines—history,

religion, philosophy, politics, literature—but their significance
lies in the very interdependence and inseparability of these manifestations of human thought and action. Two main headings that
I have adopted will, I hope, give the reader some idea of the
wealth of ideas in this essay, which Renan compared (Preface
of 1890) to a forest of thought with few clearings.

II *The Perfect Science*

It may come as a surprise to twentieth-century readers that
Renan's "scientist" is not the physical or natural scientist (though
he hopes to achieve something of their kind of "certitude"), but
the historian and philologist. Equally surprising may be the immensely broad definition he gives of "philology," which those of
us who have taken graduate courses in this field remember as a
somewhat narrowly confined and not very inspiring study of historical features of a language (morphology, phonology, etymol-
ogy, etc.). For Renan it is nothing less than "the science of the
products of the human mind." (It is significant that the work
is dedicated not to a laboratory scientist but to a professor of
Sanskrit.) The Middle Age had its saint or knight; the sixteenth
and seventeenth centuries their "perfect courtier" and "gentle-
man" (*honnête homme*); the eighteenth its man of reason or
philosophe. Renan defines his "perfect man," that is, perfect philologist, as follows: "At once poet, philosopher, scholar, and not
by intervals and at different moments ... but by intimate com-
penetration (*compénétration*) at every moment of his life, poet
while he is philosopher, philosopher while he is scholar, in
whom, in a word, all the elements of humanity would be brought
together in a superior harmony (*une harmonie supérieure*), as
in humanity itself." His goal, coinciding with "the highest degree
of intellectual culture," is nothing less than to "comprehend humanity" (*comprendre l'humanité*, a play on words, since *comprendre* means both to "understand" and to "include" or "embrace").

Though neither irreligious like Proudhon nor exclusively positivistic like Comte, the perfect scientist cannot be a believer
in any orthodox sense; belief in revelation or in the supernatural
would render his knowledge useless, his search for truth hypocritical. The "miracle" is only that which has not yet been explained: *le miracle n'est que l'inexpliqué*. However, he too will
have his way of adoring, his sense of wonderment (*admirer*);
it will simply not be blindly adoring, from a prostrate position.

His enthusiasm (*enthousiasme*, the root meaning of which is "to have God within one") will be based on knowledge and criticism. This is the meaning of Renan's dictum that only the scholar (the word in French also means scientist) has the right to admire: *le savant seul a le droit d'admirer*. A contemporary wit, Malcolm Muggeridge, has said, "We do not need to understand what we admire; if we did, how should we ever have any heroes, or even gods?" Renan's whole point is the exact opposite of this: we can truly admire only what we understand. By claiming this, he is not only suggesting a more enlightened approach to the heroes and gods of the past, but also opening up possibilities of renewed heroism and godliness for the future.

Frivolous skepticism and scholastic dogmatism are equally to be rejected: "We are critical dogmatists" (*nous sommes dogmatiques critiques*). In this choice of pronoun Renan is speaking, perhaps more than he was aware in 1848, for his generation. "We believe in truth, although we do not claim to possess absolute truth" (*nous croyons à la vérité, bien que nous ne prétendions pas posséder la vérité absolue*). These careful distinctions lead up to what is one of the most important sentences in all Renan's work, formulating a discovery that marked, for him and his generation, an advance over the Romantic position which tended to sacrifice criticism to enthusiasm or to view them as irreconcilable opposites: "Enthusiasm and the critical sense are far from excluding each other" (*L'enthousiasme et la critique sont loin de s'exclure*).

A delicate feeling for nuances, for the infinity of possibilities, is as important to the ideal scholar as the use of critical reason; the *esprit de finesse*, more important than the *esprit géométrique*. Like the genius as defined by Michelet, he is "at one and the same time simple and analytical, child and adult, man and woman, *barbare et civilisé*." For without this wonderful multiplicity of insights, he would fail to "recreate the spontaneous in the midst of the reflective" or to appreciate the contributions to humanity made by primitive peoples, by saints, geniuses, madmen—in a word, by all kinds of seers into "unknown worlds." At times Renan's contempt for what passes as "sanity" and "normality" and his interest in "intellectual monsters" (historically, part of his reaction against the long-entrenched bourgeois monarchy's spirit of conformism and mediocrity) seem to point ahead to the cult of the irrational in Rimbaud and the Surrealists. Even the child and the uncivilized man have something to teach us. Without naming child psychology and anthropology as such, he forecasts a great future for researchers into *l'enfant* and *le sauvage*, two objects of study that will become essential to "whoever would attempt to construct the scientific theory of the first ages of humanity."

Let the scholar of the future give up once and for all the vain hope of encompassing truth in a *system*, for what more is a philosophical system than its author's "epic on things" (*épopée sur les choses*), containing more poetry than truth? It is enough if our ideas are held together by *un esprit général, un esprit d'ensemble*—a valuable clue, incidentally, to the manner in which *L'Avenir de la science* itself should be read.

In practical terms, "comprehending humanity" means, for Renan, a form of historical psychology, or the attempt to portray the human spirit as revealed in writings of all kinds: collective as well as individual, popular as well as sophisticated, mediocre as well as brilliant; in myths as well as in chronicles. Religious and mythological writings, especially those which have guided whole peoples, are given the highest priority as "psychological" documents, and comparison between them advanced as the most fruitful method. Recognizing freely his debt to the pioneer *comparatiste*, Claude Fauriel, Renan champions vigorously, and again with a keen sense of the future, the study of comparative literature as well as that of comparative religions: *La comparaison est le grand instrument de la critique.*

The very word *philology* reminds us that Renan is interested above all in *written sources*. The emphasis he places on the establishment, editing, and exegesis of texts would seem at first to make him a friend of modern literary scholarship. But in the study of these texts he is far from granting priority to purely literary or esthetic criteria, as the scholarship of our own age tends to do. On the contrary, he appears to strip them of all but their value as documents revealing the human spirit. What might be called his *anti-littérature* in the *Cahiers* becomes even more extreme in this work, especially if we take the point of view of twentieth-century "close readers" or structural explicators. All kinds of corollaries that "new critics" today would find heretical flow from Renan's assumption that literature is document (that is, means) rather than artifact (end): obscure and second-rate writings are as useful to the philologist as are masterpieces; beauty comes from the epoch described, not from the description ("It is not the Homeric poem which is beautiful, but Homeric life, the phase of humanity's existence described in Homer");

most hair-raising of all, "Beauty is in things; literature is merely image and parable." [2]

But we would be poor students of Renan indeed if we failed to apply to his views on literature his own lessons on the relativity of truth and the need for historical perspective. What may appear to many to be his fallacies about literature are really part of his own "new criticism," style 1845-1849. His attacks on *rhéteurs* and *lettrés,* as he pityingly terms them, bent on seeing only the "literary aspects" of works, were justified at a time when literary study still neglected the historical origins and contexts of these same works, the traditions from which they sprang, their intellectual content.

Renan's "universal critic" will view science as being an end in itself, and the knowledge and truth it brings as corresponding to the joys of contemplation experienced by mystics. This conception bears little resemblance to the Baconian dream of science as power over nature; [3] on the contrary it is wary of technology and industry, beginning to take shape in the France of the 1840's, and contemptuous of utilitarianism, especially English. *Unum est necessarium.* Mary, the "symbol of contemplation," not her practical sister Martha, is the model of science in the Renanian sense. In one very curious respect, however, *L'Avenir de la science* does have a Baconian ring: the author's insistence on the *organization* of research, his prediction that science will advance not alone thanks to the individual genius but also to teams of researchers ("lay chapters" he calls these, and at times they take on the dignity of government-supported foundations). Even the uninspired worker will contribute a useful monograph on some special point of learning to the eventual synthesis. Yet not for Renan himself this narrow specialization, this sacrifice of broad generalization to the analysis of detail. Writing in an age of transition, when specialized knowledge was coming to be highly valued but had not yet discouraged the specialist from formulating general views of life, Renan could reasonably aim to be the *philosophe-savant.* Not for him either the reduction of learning to a professional mystery for the initiated only—least of all now that, evoking Fichte's *sacerdoce de la science,* he has become a priest of knowledge with a mission to serve humanity.

III *History, God, and Politics*

The "three age" theory borrowed from Cousin—a primitive age, religious but unscientific; an intermediate age, irreligious but scientific; a final age, both religious and scientific—provided Renan with the basic framework into which he fits his reflections on history. The first age holds the key to the mystery of mankind, just as childhood holds the key to the mystery of the individual man. The philologist Renan is less interested in man's pre-history than in his first recorded utterances, and above all, in his earliest religious and mythological systems, which provide "the embryogeny of the human spirit" (*l'embryogénie de l'esprit humain*). He salutes the searchers after spiritual origins in the newly opened fields of Indian and Oriental history, but his own projects, already firmly sketched out in two important passages to which I shall refer in the next chapter, will involve the embryological approach to the more traditional themes of Judaism and Christianity.

Whereas mankind, according to Renan, had been pictured by classical historians in terms of an absolute, fixed, static being, the great advance of nineteenth-century historical thought lies in "substituting the category of *becoming* (*devenir*) for that of *being* (*être*), the conception of the relative (*relatif*) for that of the absolute (*absolu*), and movement for immobility." Mankind's movement, I need hardly add (it is implicit in the very concept of the "three ages"), is progressive. In fact, its goal is to become God. Renan conceives of God no longer as a personal being, absolute and eternal, but as a spiritual reality emerging from human history. "What else is God for humanity," he asks, "except the transcendent sum of its spiritual needs (*le résumé transcendant de ses besoins suprasensibles*), the *category of the ideal*, the form under which we conceive the ideal, just as space and time are categories or forms under which we conceive physical bodies?" God is not, but will be. His revelation will coincide with humanity's full attainment of its rational powers (*conscience*), its complete enlightenment. Although Renan has not worked out in detail the timetable of this evolving God, he is confident that on the day when "knowledge will equal the world, and subject and object will be identified, God will be complete." The conscious, systematic hastening of that day is what Renan means, in the type of striking phrase occasionally found buried in the turgid flow of his prose, by declaring, "TO ORGANIZE HUMANITY SCIENTIFICALLY (ORGANISER SCIENTIFIQUEMENT L'HUMANITE), such is the last word of modern science, such is its bold but legitimate claim." He then adds that reason (*raison*), after organizing humanity, "WILL ORGANIZE GOD (ORGANISERA DIEU)." [4] The future of science is the future of God.

However, Renan's variation on what is clearly recognizable as the eighteenth-century theme of progress and perfectibility involves a number of important qualifications. Progress is a matter not of simple, irresistible forward march, but of "oscillations," each advance being followed by a temporary setback. Humanity moves toward perfection through a succession of imperfect forms. Two types of imagery occur in this context: history is a tapestry being woven by workers who, since they work from the back of the cloth, cannot always see the pattern they are weaving; it is also a digestive system in which waste is inevitable and which is able to absorb errors and crimes into itself while remaining healthy.[5]

We touch here on Renan's political views. Conservative, even reactionary, measures and beliefs that seem to block progress in a given period are, he claims, often salutary means of checking a dangerously accelerated *marche*, or, we might put it, of preventing a fatal case of indigestion. Given this theory, even the Inquisition becomes an instrument of progress. Yet, revolution is no less necessary than conservatism. In *L'Avenir de la science,* as the very subtitle, *pensées de 1848,* implies, Renan has encountered the idea of revolution. He has discovered that 1789 marks a turning point in history: before, all was politically fatalistic and irrational; after, the idea has been launched that rational men are capable of taking their destinies in their own hands, and the world can never be the same for this idea. He has also discovered the socialism of the Comte de Saint-Simon (*saint-simonisme*), one of the most ambitious nineteenth-century programs to reorganize society, in this case by the cooperation of various élites consisting of scholars, artists, industrialists, and financiers.

Renan's attitude toward revolutionary republicanism and socialism in *L'Avenir de la science* is profoundly ambiguous. His personal background partly accounts for this ambiguity. Of plebeian origins, he is hardly insincere when he declares that "genius" must be rooted in the people (*le génie est peuple,* another echo of Michelet). As a seminarian, he had been deeply influenced by the ambiguity of Catholicism itself toward democracy. Though its teaching that we are all equal in the sight of God has democratic implications, its priesthood sets apart some men as "more equal than others," marks them as an élite to represent God and to rule spiritually. The very concept of the priest-

hood is, if not undemocratic, at least paternalistic, tending to
reflect the paternalism inherent in Christian theism itself. Renan's
political philosophy, as formulated in 1848-1849, merely trans-
lates into terms of his new scientific religion this ambivalent
Catholic position. Although he is aware that the masses exist,
recognizes that the improvement of their material lot is essential
to their spiritual progress, and even holds out hope of self-
government for them, he distrusts them. He argues, furthermore,
that a benevolent authoritarian rule may be called for in France
until Frenchmen are truly ready for republicanism—a type of
reasoning which comes dangerously close to one of the classic
forms of the rationalization of dictatorship.

Of the trinity of sacred revolutionary slogans, Renan admits
the utility of *liberté* and *fraternité*, but has no use for *égalité*.
The masses may be part of humanity, but they are not responsible for its highest achievements; their inequality (political, social, economic) may in fact be a condition of those achievements.
Versailles is impossible without the underprivileged. In any
given age it will be the privileged élite rather than the broad
mass of human beings who will express most perfectly the human capacity for truth and beauty.[6] The fundamental political
problem for Renan, first set forth in *L'Avenir de la science*, is to
determine by what instrumentality the work of the élite can be
furthered. Something of the privileged position of the clergy in
the Catholic religion persists in this aristocratic ideal; priests
and monks merely give way to "scientists." But the ideal also
stems from Greek antiquity, as Renan reveals in a formula not
calculated to reassure partisans of the most broadly based political democracy: his perfect society is "Greece without slavery"
(*la Grèce sans esclavage*).

A more serious obstacle to Renan's espousal of the revolutionary cause, whether it be 1848 or *saint-simonisme*, is his fear
that the very idea of political action may be incompatible with
the exercise of the critical faculty. The philosopher weakens, if
not defiles, himself by what we would today call political *en-
gagement*, especially in a specifically partisan cause. *L'homme
politique* comes off even worse in *L'Avenir de la science* than
the *littérateur*. Renan's reasoning here, borrowed from Herder,
is simple, in fact too simple: for the politician, man is a *means;*
for the moral thinker (and the true critic is a moral thinker), he
is an *end*. The "revolution of the future" will consist of the "triumph of morality over politics" (*le triomphe de la morale sur
la politique*).

I owe it to Renan to emphasize at this point that these "thoughts of 1848," politically speaking, have little finality about them. In no part of the work is the author's thinking in a greater state of flux and contradiction than in his political ideas. What is expressed here is the first phase of a long evolution by virtue of which Renan will overcome, though perhaps never completely, both his prejudice against popular government and his prejudice against political action for the thinker.

IV A *Youthful Dream Reclaimed*

In the *Cahiers de jeunesse* Renan had spoken of a "combat of content and form" (*combat du fond et de la forme*) which prevented his harmonizing science with religion more perfectly in his work. *L'Avenir de la science,* though obviously too ill-defined and unpolished to resolve this conflict successfully, is, nevertheless, cast in a form (however formless in appearance) that is curiously well suited to its purposes. It is the expression of an initially Romantic Renan, creator of a fruitful chaos of ideas from which the mature Renan will draw generously in the composition of better balanced, calmer, more classical structures of thought. What is revolutionary about the work is not this or that idea but the total impression it gives of feverish struggle to reach a better order—religious, political, literary—than the traditional order, symbolized by the complacent materialism and timid conservatism of the July Monarchy. "Woe to the generation which has known only a policy tied to rules (*une police régulière*), and which has conceived life as repose and art as enjoyment (*qui a conçu la vie comme un repos et l'art comme une jouissance*)."

The openness and formlessness of the work lend support to its theme of futurity. "Order is an end, not a beginning" (*L'ordre est une fin, non un commencement*)—a superb motto in any age for youth's resistance against being forced by elders into a mold not of its making. The very contradictions that seem to flower out naturally in the work, with little effort on the author's part to reconcile them, the *insolubles antinomies*—rational versus irrational; perfect knowledge versus persistent mystery; aristocracy versus democracy; humanity as center of the universe versus humanity as mere epiphenomenon—are all part of the emerging order of things. Contradiction, as in Hegel, is envisioned as blessing rather than evil, thus establishing a major theme of Renan's work as a whole. "The life of humanity, like that of the individual, rests upon necessary contradictions" (*La vie de l'humanité, comme la vie de l'individu, pose sur des contradictions nécessaires*). To eliminate from *L'Avenir de la science* all that is unstable, unsettled, provisional, or transitional in the formulation of its ideas would be to destroy its very theme.

Something of an awareness that these apparent "faults" of his first major work were really virtues must have motivated Renan to publish it in 1890, almost half a century after writing it. In his Preface of that year he is concerned, not, as we are, with analyzing the work in its own right, but with explaining its delayed publication and comparing his views in 1890 to his views in 1848. Above all, he wishes to reclaim what is still true in his beliefs of 1848. His resurrection of this work was an act of great shrewdness. With a reaction going full strong in the 1880's and 1890's against the cult of science (known in France as *scientisme*), it was his way of reaffirming his faith in science while setting forth honest qualifications that removed all suggestion of dogmatism from that faith. He removed the *isme* but kept the *science*. Besides, there was a touch of deviltry, characteristic of the post-Franco-Prussian-War Renan, in his revelation of this work. Having enjoyed, in so many of his later publications, shocking those who thought correctly and respectably (the *bien pensants* of the Third Republic), he would now shock his more frivolous followers with a work of absolutely fervent, even painfully intense, idealism.

But he also reaches out, in both Preface and text, to the youth of 1890, and in a sense to future generations of youth. His retrospective remarks on both content and style are offered as much in defense of youthful insight as in self-criticism. The precise note he would strike is that of readjustment of his dreams to more modest scale without disheartening his younger readers. His optimism of 1848 may have been exaggerated, but "on the whole I was right" (*En somme, j'avais raison*). Inequality of individuals and races may be a more permanent part of the human condition than he realized; yet educating the masses (*culture extensive*), if only to preserve them from religious fanaticism, is as important as the cultivation of an élite (*culture intensive*). Science may "preserve from error" more than it gives truth; human destiny may seem, ironically, to grow more obscure as scientific knowledge accumulates, and men to grow more foolish politically as they mature intellectually. However, less certain though he now is in 1890 of the coming age—the third and final —of full enlightenment, he still believes in the purposeful direction of history. A "secret spring-work" (*un ressort secret*) guides humanity; if its progress is no longer the confident epic of 1848, it still has design and meaning, like those hidden in an "obscure painting" (*un canevas obscur*). Hegel may have erred, he points out, in attributing the central role in the universe to humanity; human history may have no more importance than the moss or lichen gathered on a humid surface; yet human history must keep its primacy if only because "humanity alone, so far as we know, creates the conscience of the universe."

What Renan says of style in his Preface also partakes of this subtle mixture of cautious amendment of error and fervent encouragement to youth. The awkwardness of his expression at twenty-five, his ineptness in the "art of composition," the weightiness of these burdened branches of thought forking in all directions—all these faults he freely acknowledges. But in a curious echoing of his criticism of conventional elegance of expression and of *littérature* already noted in the *Cahiers de jeunesse*, he again regrets that "to write" is "to limit oneself" (*écrire, c'est se borner*), to blunt the edge of one's thought (*émousser*, the very verb echoes across half a century from *Cahiers* to Preface). And this loss is all the more inescapable if one writes in French and must sacrifice completeness and depth of thought to that language's tyrannical exigencies of "clarity," forcing one's ideas into its "mold of well made sentences" (*le moule des phrases bien faites*).

V *In Search of L'Oeuvre*

Yet for all the ironic regret which Renan expresses in the Preface of *L'Avenir de la science* for having sacrificed the full expression of his thought to the taste of refined readers (*les gens du monde, le monde littéraire*, whom he opposes to the young, *les jeunes*), it is unthinkable that he would have continued to write in the manner of this early work. Unique though it is for the moving image it gives us of a young man confronting himself (*en face de soi*) and thinking out his thoughts in isolation (*qui pensait seul avec lui-même*), it is not the work of an artist. The word "style" derives from *stylus*, a sharply pointed instrument used by the Romans to write on wax tablets; it is related to "styletto," a small dagger. Thus, the significance of Renan's comparison of his unformed style in the *Cahiers* to a *poignard* (dagger) covered with a veil, lacking sharpness. *L'Avenir de la science*, in his words, is written with repeated hammer blows (*coups de marteau*), rather than with a stylus. The author's theoretical awareness of the need for nuances and subtleties is greater than his practical command of a style suited to their expression.

Furthermore, the work lacks an essential element of the Renanian synthesis: the beautiful. The word *beau* occurs very frequently in the *Cahiers,* often referring to the reconciliation of *science* and *esthétique,* the *beau synthétique,* which Renan longs to achieve. *L'Avenir de la science* continues to refer to this *œuvre synthétique,* this supreme work of synthesis; but it is not in itself *l'œuvre,* or even, strictly speaking, *une œuvre.* The force of both these early writings lies in their being a repertory of themes to be developed, as well as in being the spectacle of a young *échappé de séminaire* proving to himself that he could be a scholar, a philosopher, even a poet, without sacrifice of spiritual dignity and plenitude. The author of *L'Avenir de la science,* as Jean Guéhenno so well puts it, is "a young Faust" striving to know the "human equation" as thoroughly as a priest would know his God.[7]

The Renan for whom truth has many angles and many faces is already present in both *Cahiers* and *L'Avenir de la science,* and therefore almost, but not quite, the essential and complete Renan. He is very close, however, to the "framework of knowledge" (*le cadre de la science*) large enough to permit his genius to deploy all its gifts in the true *œuvre de synthèse.*

CHAPTER 4

Porticoes to theMonumental Work

PREDESTINATION to the priesthood was a fate which Renan successfully shook off. Another form of predestination he was happy to embrace: that which made him a historian. The word *histoire* in French means "story" as well as "history," and it was from the hearing of innumerable stories of the Breton saints— mixtures of legend and historical fact buried deep in the popular memory—that his boyhood imagination took the spark of a life-long vocation. "This strange environment gave me whatever qualifications I may possess for historical studies. I took from it the habit of seeing underground and discerning sounds which other ears do not hear. The essence of criticism is the ability to understand states of mind far different from that in which we live. I have seen the primitive world." [1] But even if Renan had not been a Breton, breathing ancient history in the very air, he might have been predisposed toward a sense of history by the fact of being (or having been) a Christian. "Christianity," it has been said, "is a religion of historians." [2] Looking back we note as significant that he took a second prize in history at Saint-Nicolas du Chardonnet, and that he exchanged one prize book, *The Preacher's Library,* for another, Bossuet's *Histoire des variations des églises protestantes.* Bossuet and Michelet, two historians with a strong conviction that history has a purpose, in other words with a bent for "finalism" similar to that which we find in Renan himself, were among his favored authors as a seminarian.

I *Growth of a Vocation*

A "sense of history," however, does not suffice for the budding historian. He must also possess specialized qualifications. These, too, Renan began very early to acquire. The arduous discipline of Hebrew philology was the first such approach to history he mastered, thanks to Abbé Le Hir: "*M. Le Hir fixa ma vie. J'étais philologue d'instinct*" (*Souvenirs d'enfance et de jeunesse*). Somewhat later, epigraphy, or the science of interpreting inscriptions, and archaeology were added to the skills which served as precious auxiliaries to his historical research.

Despite the element of truth existing in Renan's memory of being a "born historian," he did not proceed to this vocation without having first eliminated other possibilities. An enormous letter to Henriette (December 15, 1845) shows him, true to that search for the broadest framework possible for his talents, which we have noted as a theme of his early writings, dismissing, first, "literature which is only literature," then, the physical sciences, as too little philosophical, and settling, finally, upon *l'histoire et la haute littérature critique* as worthiest of his attention. What good is it, he asks, for a man to be "learned about nature" (*savant dans la nature*), if he is not "learned about himself and about God," if he is not, in a word, a philosopher? And history for him, as it was for Schlegel, Kant, and Hegel, is philosophy; indeed, the highest and most valid form of philosophy. The only problem remaining was the selection of a historical specialty. His choice of Semitic studies showed characteristic practicality; he sized it up as a field in which French specialists were not yet overabundant, as in Greek or Oriental studies, and, therefore, one in which his success could be greater, especially if he turned to what he considered a neglected part of the Semitic field, the comparative study of Hebrew and the classical languages.

Though there is evidence that Renan conceived, as early as 1845, of the idea of writing a history of the origins of Christianity (I shall return to the relevant texts later), he prepared himself for this immense task very gradually, by way of a number of historical exercises in more specialized fields. In fact, his Volney Prize work, *L'Histoire des langues sémitiques* (1847) and the publication of the first volume of *Les Origines du christianisme*, that is, the *Vie de Jésus* (1863), are separated by almost twenty years. In addition to his history of Semitic languages, he published during these two decades a general essay on the birth of language, *De l'origine du langage* (1848); his doctoral dissertation, *Averroès et l'averroïsme* (1852); a collection of periodical essays, *Etudes d'histoire religieuse* (1857); and two translations, with commentaries, of Old Testament works, *Le Livre de Job* (1858) and *Le Cantique des Cantiques*, or *Song of Songs* (1860). Renan himself considered all these works as so many vestibules or porticoes (*propylées* is the learned term he uses) to the main structure he was building.[3] Excusing himself, in a letter to Berthelot of October 4, 1860, for being "the least epistolary of men," especially with those of whose affection he was sure, he wrote: "Until I have done my *Origins of Christianity,* I shall be like an owl, and shall give myself only parsimoniously to letter writing and conversation. You have finished your monument; I have only completed the propylaea of mine." This would seem justification enough for treating such works very briefly, and less in themselves than for the manner in which they prepare us for his *opus magnum.*

In his *Histoire des langues sémitiques,* Renan undertakes to do for Semitic languages what the great German philologist Franz Bopp had done for Indo-European languages, namely, a comparative study of their broad traits. What began as a purely factual comparative grammar was enlarged, very characteristically, into a theoretical discussion of the role of Semitic languages in the "history of the human spirit." Anticipating in striking fashion his method as a historian of religions, Renan defends the historian's right to go beyond "purely material facts" and to make "conjectures," as well as to state frankly the contradictions and obscurities that are an inevitable part of history. For the most part a highly technical work, it nevertheless contains much of interest for the nonspecialist, since it is actually a portrait of the Semitic genius as expressed in its languages. With the Indo-European gifts for the rational pursuits of science and philosophy, Renan contrasts the superior Semitic instinct for religion, elaborating his controversial theory that "the desert is monotheistic" (*le désert est monothéiste*). For all the impersonality of this learned work, it is obvious that Renan himself is strongly attracted to this "simple patriarchal religion, without mysticism, without subtle theology, bordering on incredulity."

De l'origine du langage, though much shorter, is much broader in scope. It is Renan's first practical exercise in the "embryogeny of the human spirit." (Whole sentences are borrowed from the unpublished manuscript of *L'Avenir de la science,* in which he had discussed this "embryogeny" more theoretically.) Language he views as the "monument" or "poem" of primitive man; and he is concerned to refute both the theological claim that language is divinely revealed and the eighteenth-century rationalist claim that language is deliberately invented. Like religion, language is the unreflective, intuitive creation of a whole people acting collectively and impersonally, though this anonymous creation may be "personified" or guided in its development by an élite. Language cannot be radically altered, but develops according to its own laws like the oak from the acorn; the comparison of language with vegetation occurs frequently and is worth stressing, since it will later have its analogy in the explanation of how Christianity grew out of Judaism. Renan makes much use of German sources, especially of the pioneer work in comparative philology by Jacob Grimm. Indeed Grimm stands in relation to this historical analysis of language somewhat as the Biblical scholar David Strauss will stand in relation to *Vie de Jésus*. But the error should be corrected once and for all that Renan follows his German sources slavishly; he is as freely critical of Grimm as he will be of Strauss, sometimes giving to their views an independent twist, sometimes rejecting them outright and replacing them with his own.

Renan's doctoral dissertation, *Averroès et l'averroïsme*, on the subject of the great twelfth-century Spanish-born Arab philosopher, best known for his interpretation of Aristotle, is a much more significant step than his linguistic studies toward his major work.[4] At first glance, at least to the layman, the connection with Judeo-Christian history seems remote. The anti-Semitism rife among Arabs has caused us to forget that Arabic is itself a Semitic language spoken by Semitic peoples. To elucidate many phenomena of Jewish and Christian history, Renan will draw on parallels with Arabic cultures. "It is only a few days journey," he reminds us, "from Jerusalem to Sinai and from Sinai to Mecca." Points of contact between the three religions are constantly being established in his work. Before becoming the historian of the Jewish form of Semitic faith, Renan is the historian of forms of rationalism and incredulity among Semitic peoples. He describes his *Averroès* quite simply as "a history of incredulity in the Middle Ages" (letter to Berthelot, March 31, 1850).

Subtitled *essai historique*, this thesis is indeed the first major testing of his originality as a historian, the trying-out of a number of attitudes and techniques that he will adopt in his central work. The type of historical work which *Averroès* represents had already been foreshadowed in a passage in the *Cahiers de jeunesse* calling for a new kind of biography of great men, their "life beyond the tomb, their influence, their various fortunes, the manner in which they have shaped other minds. . . ." Today, as "influence study," this is an acquired fact; in 1845 there was some originality in suggesting such a project, and even more merit in 1852 in carrying it out successfully. In tracing the posthumous influence of Averroès, the manner in which he became a symbol and in which his ideas were both preserved and distorted, Renan is preparing the ground for a much more controversial biography, the "posthumous biogaphy" of Jesus.[5]

Apart from these claims to significance as a "historical essay," *Averroès* seems to me to possess at least three others. To begin with, Renan proves his ability for the first time to write with sympathy—a sympathy tinged characteristically with irony, to be sure—of beliefs which he finds false and at times absurd, but which he respects because they are part of the "tableau of the successive evolutions of the human spirit." And this paradoxical attitude rests with firm logic upon his conviction that humanity thinking out its problems is a worthy phenomenon to contemplate, *per se*, even though the solutions it proposes at given times are to be rejected. "One is a historian only on condition that one can reproduce at will in oneself different types of past life...." Secondly, unlike the essays in philological history, Renan is here handling extensively and interpreting, for the first time, as every historian must, original documents. The very word "document" is used repeatedly, with proud awareness, in the Preface. The privilege of drawing on such primary sources Renan owed to the mission he carried out in 1849 and 1850 in Italy— the first of many "field trips" for this historian—the purpose of which was to catalogue Syrian and Arabic manuscripts in Italian libraries and archives. This leads to the third and final point. *Averroès* is the first fruit of Renan's discovery, thanks to the "unbending" that Italy caused in his rigid Northern nature, of "the artistic side of life," a discovery rich in implications for his entire work.[6] The pre-*Averroès* or pre-Italian Renan is convinced that beauty must be a part of the great work of synthesis he is undertaking, but he is acquainted with beauty only in the abstract. Now, converted to the reality of art, he has progressed beyond the merely elegant style of his earlier historical works to the first of his books which we can call both learned and beautifully written. A more pronounced enemy than ever of Scholastic logic and "rational" demonstration, taking the Italian Renaissance humanists as his models, Renan enunciates a major tenet of his method as historian and philosopher: "Form, in philosophy, is at least as important as content; the turn given to one's thought is its only possible proof" (*le tour donné à la pensée est la seule démonstration possible*).

In his studies of the Book of Job and the Song of Songs, which bring us to the threshold of *Vie de Jésus*, Renan came to grips with the "strangeness" of the "Hebrew spirit" (as he calls it) in what is perhaps the best way possible: by translation, and more precisely by having to translate from a language in his opinion recalcitrant to "rational" and "logical" thought, in the

Western sense, into a language that passes as the epitome of logic and rationality. Once again, as with his work on Averroès, curiously enough, he seems to be skirting the more traditional and orthodox theme of the God of Israel, sparring with it before the serious duel begins.

The Book of Job he calls the "ideal Semitic poem," a mirror of the Semitic, rather than of the specifically Jewish, spirit.[7] As for its place in the Old Testament canon, he interprets it, along with the Book of Ecclesiastes, as a moment of questioning and doubt, in the midst of the more characteristically Jewish affirmative and prophetic spirit. He is attracted to it both for its content—the great theme of the just man seeking a transcendent reason for his just behavior, a metaphysical validation for his goodness (a theme with lasting personal meaning for Renan himself)—and for its form, the dialectic which proceeds, as Renan himself prefers, by "lively intuitions rather than by logical deductions," the dialogue which freely admits necessary contradictions and reaches no real conclusion, since the problem it raises may be insoluble.

The Song of Songs, a creation of a "young Israel of the time of the patriarchs," before Israel became "the people of God," is for Renan a profane, though not a frivolous, book, an *œuvre de distraction,* arising not from a "moment of doubt," like Job or Ecclesiastes, but from a "moment of forgetfulness." In the introductory study of the plan, age, and character of this enigmatic work, Renan provides a brilliant example of what the French call an *état présent,* or essay in the survey of research in a given field. He also defends his interpretation of the work as a five-act play set in a harem and concerned with triangular love; he denies, as a philological error, the orthodox Catholic view of this poem as a mystical allegory, though taking pains to explain how such a view, historically false, may nevertheless not be completely devoid of religious truth.

A Semiticist in the broadest sense before he is a Hebraist and historian of Judaism and Christianity, Renan, as though reluctant to tackle head-on his major subject, first sharpens his skills as a philologist and then sidles up to his central theme by broad essays on the world outlook of the Semitic peoples as mirrored in their language, by the study of the "rational mysticism" and incredulity of a great Arab philosopher, and by meditations on "profane works," somewhat heterodox and a-typical, marginal to the great religious vocation of Judaism—the troubling philosophical drama of *Job,* the pastoral-erotic *Song of Songs.* Another way of considering this approach is to view it as the prudent testing of a critical method. Renan first applies his method to more or less neutral subjects in philological and philosophical history, and then moves cautiously toward introducing it into the very inner sanctum of the most controversial theme in religious history.

II *The* Opus Magnum *and Its Genesis*

Renan was forty when he published *Vie de Jésus,* the first of seven books constituting *Les Origines du christianisme,* the last of which is *Marc-Aurèle et la fin du monde antique,* published in 1882. An average interval of three years occurred between the appearance of these different parts. The ten years between *Marc-Aurèle* and his death in 1892 Renan devoted primarily to *Histoire du peuple d'Israël,* consisting of five "tomes" (ten books or *livres*), the first brought out in 1887 (he was then sixty-four) and the last posthumously in 1893. Almost forty years of labor, from his "second maturity" at the age of forty to his death at sixty-nine; twelve volumes of history, covering over five thousand pages in the spacious original edition, and spanning over twelve centuries of narrative—no wonder that Renan spoke of this subject as making up the center of a life's reflections (*le centre de mes réflexions*). Logically, as well as chronologically, he ought to have begun with the history of the Jewish people. "But life is short and of uncertain duration. I was pressed for time: I threw myself into the midst of the subject, and began with the life of Jesus, assuming the prior revolutions of Jewish religion to be known." [8] In esthetic terms (and this dual work forms an esthetic as well as a historical whole), *Histoire du peuple d'Israël* is an immense, long-delayed flashback, in which the ripened fruit of the Gospel is traced back to the seed planted in the eighth century B.C. by the prophet Isaiah, "the first founder of Christianity."

The "embryogeny" of this work—to apply to it a key concept in Renan's own interpretation of history—may be uncovered in several pages of his youthful writings. These seminal passages are also important for the way they reveal the whole spirit in which the work was conceived, as well as its fundamental purpose. In the first such text, dating from 1845 (*Cahiers*), Renan notes his reactions to a conversation in which two "rationalist" professors (Garnier and Havet) equate Christianity with superstition and credulity: "What stupidity! ... I myself no longer believe, but ... if one must, to be an unbeliever in Christianity,

say such nonsense, then I will have none of it." A few lines later
we find the true kernel from which his life's work will grow:
"Who," he asks, "will give me the power to do a book on Christianity, which will tell in definitive manner how one ought finally
to consider it!" (*un livre du christianisme, qui dira définitivement
comment il est temps de le prendre*).

Renan's "book on Christianity" is thus clearly to be a reply to
"incredulity" of this short-sighted kind; he will praise, even exalt,
Christianity, when appropriate; but above all, he will "humanize"
it (*je l'humaniserai*). Voltaire was wrong to ridicule; Chateaubriand, wrong to see only the *beau* and the *poétique*. Yet "both
are right" (*les deux ont raison*); the truth must take account of
both negative and positive aspects of such a complex phenomenon.

Conceived still in somewhat vague terms in the *Cahiers*, the
great project is more explicitly formulated in *L'Avenir de la
science*. Furthermore, its fundamental thesis—the Jewishness of
the Christian religion—is already firmly posited. "The most important book of the nineteenth century," he writes, "should have
as its title *Histoire critique des origines du christianisme*." If
fate allows, he goes on to say, it will be the work of his own
maturity, and, against those who claim that Christianity originated from a fusion of Oriental, Platonic, and Jewish elements,
he will prove that it was "originally a Jewish fact" (*primitivement un fait juif*), however much its subsequent history may
have obscured its Jewish origins.

Another passage of *L'Avenir de la science* makes clear Renan's
conviction that the author best qualified to write the history of
Christianity, in fact the history of any religion, is one who has
been, but no longer is, a believer. "Those can understand Christ
who have believed in him; to understand fully any sublime religious creations, one must have believed in them (*il faudrait y
avoir cru*), or rather (for the word 'to believe' [*croire*] has no
sense in such a world of imagination), one must have lived with
them." [9] "Generally speaking," he concludes, "one can be sure
that when a work of the human spirit appears too absurd or
bizarre, it is because it has been misunderstood or falsely viewed.
If we placed ourselves in the right light, we would see the reason for it" (*on en verrait la raison*).

CHAPTER 5

Comedy of History

O NE would see the reason for it"—this phrase quoted at the end of the last chapter is of immense importance. The whole point of Renan's historical research is not to prove that Christianity is true or false (in any case, hardly the task of a historian), but to explain how it came about. This motivation should be kept clearly in mind as we turn now to survey *Les Origines du christianisme* and *Histoire du peuple d'Israël*, the first of which Edmund Wilson has called "a masterpiece—perhaps the greatest of all histories of ideas," [1] and both of which constitute, without doubt, one of the most ambitious historical works ever undertaken by a French author.

I *The Galilean Reality*

The first paragraph of Chapter One of *Vie de Jésus* ("The Place of Jesus in World History") states three ideas that will govern the entire *Origines du christianisme:* first, the "revolution" of Christianity is "the principal event in the history of the world"; second, this revolution required almost a thousand years to be achieved, that is, seven centuries to emerge from its Jewish antecedents and almost three centuries to establish itself as a "new religion"; and third, its immediate origins date from the reigns of Augustus and Tiberius, its founder being "a superior person" (*une personne supérieure*).

For the historical fact supporting this third idea Renan relies on the Synoptic Gospels and, to a lesser extent, on the Fourth Gospel.[2] Much less of a skeptic in this respect than Strauss or the liberal French Protestant exegetes, he believes that the Gospels have some historical validity; his narrative is based on an attempt to disengage history from legend in these sources. Under the heading of "legend" he classifies all the "miracles," on the a priori ground that the "miracle," understood as the specific intervention of a superhuman power in the operation of nature, is an impossibility. Jesus is "miraculous" only in the

sense that he is governed by a fresh and powerful religious instinct, a primitive psychology with laws of its own, befitting the
"childhood of humanity" and lost to modern men in a reflective
and analytical age. But strangely different though his nature
may be from ours, he remains bound by nature; he is a *miracle
psychologique*.[3]

Traditional Catholic "lives" of Jesus had tended to be long
on dogma and apologetics, and short on history. In fact, to term
them "lives" at all may be a misnomer: the Protestant religious
historian, Maurice Goguel, calls Renan's "the first *Vie de Jésus*
to appear in a Catholic country." [4] Renan's Jesus is rooted in his
race, his country, and his time, very much like the Racine or
Byron of Taine's literary criticism; the difference lies in his degree of greatness and influence. He is a Jew, the perfect fruit of
a long race of Jewish prophets, but his vision of goodness is
shaped by the gentle pastoral beauty of the Galilean landscape,
in contrast with the harsh landscape of Jerusalem. Galilee and
Jerusalem are the positive and negative poles of this biography.
The *Vie de Jésus*, unique in this way among all the books of
the Judeo-Christian cycle, is cast as a pure idyll or pastoral.
Serenity and joyousness, even gaiety, prevail. The sadness and
suffering of Holy Week come as a kind of surprise, jarring with
all that precedes. It has been said that Renan's Jesus has the
flaw of being a mirror of Renan, and there is some truth in the
charge. Yet in a number of important respects there is sharp
dissimilarity between the historian and his subject, most strikingly in the fact that Jesus, unlike his historian, is not a learned
man (*un savant*). To have ascribed to Jesus the limited knowledge, indeed the errors, of his age was perhaps Renan's most
audacious stroke.[5]

The greatness of Jesus, for Renan, lies in his having given
perfect, definitive expression to the age-old Hebrew dream of a
universal religion of the spirit, without rites, doctrine, or ex-
ternal forms. He is the supreme *ébionite*, or believer in the
brotherhood and moral equality of all men, including the poor
and the lowly. Politically conservative (a feature his disciples
will perpetuate), he is, in his preaching against the rich and
respectable, socially revolutionary, in fact anarchistic. But above
all—these are the epithets that recur most often—he is gentle
(*doux*), delightful (*délicieux*), charming (*charmant, ravissant*).
Renan has been ridiculed for his excessive use, if not abuse, of
the adjective *charmant* applied to the Saviour. However, his use
of this word is less absurd if we recall the full force of its

etymological meaning, most probably the sense in which he intended it, namely, "enchanting," "bewitching," characterized by magic power over others. A modern historian might be inclined to say "charismatic." [6]

II *Deification*

The life of Jesus ends, for Renan, with his death on the cross. But this event merely gives further impetus to a process already begun during his lifetime: his deification. Renan had attempted to explain the "miracles" of Jesus as pious inventions of his disciples, or thaumaturgical acts exaggerated out of all proportion. In a manner consistent with this interpretation, he considers the greatest "miracle" attributed to Jesus—his own resurrection—as a legend arising from the understandable enthusiasm of his disciples (initially, from the "hysteria" of Mary Magdalene), who could not accept his mortality, who must, out of their love for him, "do violence to reality." Jesus, he claims, did not believe he was God, but allowed his disciples so to believe.

The transformation of a great religious leader into a God is, for Renan, a recurring pattern of religious history, having almost the force of a law. His pages on the psychology behind the creation of such divine legends are, of course, vital to his argument. The terms he uses ("pious fraud," etc.) are really inadequate, for they still suggest, despite all his careful qualifications, trickery or deceit—the very Voltairian argument he is in fact rejecting. But, although his vocabulary may fail him here, Renan's intentions are clear: the error and proneness to illusion he ascribes to Jesus' disciples are part of that "primitive psychology" for which *L'Avenir de la science* and the earlier philological works have already prepared us, a concrete application of his theory, by now familiar to us, of "humanity's childhood." Falsification of reality on the part of these sublime idealists becomes a kind of creative ignorance, an "illness" raised to the level where "the words healthy and ill are completely relative"—a generous interpretation to which, one need hardly add, Voltaire would not have subscribed. [7]

No life of Christ will ever satisfy everyone. Subjective feeling comes into play in this field, at least for those raised in Judeo-Christian traditions, with a power that it never has, say, when one judges a history of transportation or a history of the sonnet. For all those readers who find Renan's *Vie de Jésus* superficial, distasteful, or shocking, if not blasphemous, there will be as many who find it moving and its portion of truth substantial. The author himself, as he states in his final chapter, firmly believed that his critical approach, by "humanizing" Jesus, restored to him a greater dignity. It seems unfair to dismiss this opening volume of his historical cycle, as many have done, as merely a "novel" or a "poem." Once allowance has been made for the paucity and fragility of the historical sources available and for the probably insuperable difficulties involved in what Albert Schweitzer calls "the quest for the historical Jesus," Renan is essentially attempting in this work no more and no less than what any good historian attempts: to create an image of the past in which he can believe. And Renan can accept a Jesus who is "divine" only in the sense that he brought humanity closer than ever before to the "concept of the divine." The true flaw of his *Vie de Jésus* is not that it is "unhistorical" but that it is partial and one-sided. One wonders, above all, how such a gentle dreamer managed to end up on Calvary.

III   *The Apostles and Saint Paul's Christian Odyssey*

In *Les Apôtres* (1866) and *Saint Paul* (1869), with the *Acts of the Apostles* and the Pauline Epistles as his major sources, Renan moves onto more solidly historical ground.[8] The first of these books, compared with *Vie de Jésus*, may strike the reader as somewhat sober, if not dry, in tone. The main burden of the argument is to relate how the "Galilean reality" (*la réalité galiléenne*), the person of Jesus who remains "the true founder of Christianity," continues to be deified, by virtue of what Renan calls "a contagion of vision." Christianity shapes its legends and takes on an admixture of superstition which he attributes to ineradicable pagan traits in its early adherents.

Vie de Jésus, essentially a biography, has a kind of simplified, in fact oversimplified, unity to it. With *Les Apôtres* we begin to perceive that skillful interweaving of parallel tableaux which Renan will gradually bring to perfection as a major technique of his historical art. Chapter XVIII, "The State of the World Toward the Middle of the First Century," a central chapter, is a fine example of this kind of broad survey of collective beliefs and states of mind, in a given era, in which Renan excels. Three "worlds" are linked together: the Christian, the Jewish, the Greco-Roman. The major themes of this manifold tableau are: the continuing bond of early Christianity with Judaism, or, in other words, the coexistence of two Judaisms, the *judaïsme phari-*

saïque and the *judaïsme libre,* which will be a constituent element of Christianity; second, the convent-like communities of
the early churches, out of which monastic life, an essential in-
gredient of Christianity in Renan's eyes, will grow; and finally,
the limitations of Greek and Roman ideals (*la froide cellule du
temple païen*) in their competition with the more vital religious
spirit of church and synagogue.

If Renan has little enthusiasm for the Apostles, his fervor
rekindles in his extraordinary *Saint Paul,* the matter of which he
envisions as an "unequalled epic," the "Christian Odyssey," a
story which he is impatient to recount to us. Like *Vie de Jésus,*
this is a strongly topographical book; the early editions appended
to the title the phrase "with a map of Saint Paul's voyages."
Renan must be one of the few historians to have followed in the
steps of Paul throughout his Mediterranean missions. Once again,
as with *Vie de Jésus,* a *compagne fidèle* accompanied him; no
longer his sister this time (she had died and lay buried in Syria),
but his wife, Cornélie Scheffer. The book is dedicated to her,
as *Vie de Jésus* had been dedicated to Henriette. "Together we
have seen Ephesus and Antioch, Philippi and Thessalonica,
Athens and Corinth, Colossae and Laodicea." (The French original is so much more musical: *Nous avons vu ensemble Ephèse et
Antioche, Philippes et Thessalonique, Athènes et Corinthe, Co-
losses et Laodicée.*) Unlike the portrait of Jesus, however, the
portrait of Paul is multi-dimensional. It has those complexities
and contradictions which, as Renan himself so often tells us, are
inseparable from life. A sense for them is surely also essential
to the writing of great history. Their absence, perhaps deliberate,
from *Vie de Jésus,* weakens that book. If *Saint Paul,* on the
other hand, is, as I believe it is, the most forceful and deeply
felt of all the volumes in *Les Origines du christianisme,* the reason is also because it is written neither with detachment nor out
of pure love or pure hatred, but with the mixture of respect and
distrust, admiration and censure, that often brings a historical
subject alive.

Renan's Saint Paul is a symbol of the "man of action," as opposed to the "man of contemplation." There is in Renan himself,
as we have seen in *L'Avenir de la science,* a distrust of the man
of action; but there is also a profound desire to be precisely
such a man, an apostle somehow reconciling action with intelligence, faith with critical sense. In 1869, frustrated in his attempts to exercise direct political influence (his unsuccessful
electoral campaign for a deputyship), and only a year away from

the national débâcle of 1870, Renan the historian begins to betray
signs of an increasing weight of disappointment, an increasing
skepticism concerning the sane conduct or wise reform of human
affairs. This weight will be felt in all the subsequent volumes
until it is again lifted in *Histoire du peuple d'Israël* and Renan,
recharged by long contact with the Hebrew prophets, returns to
a kind of transposed and modernized messianic spirit.[9] Saint
Paul is the "hero of action," the hero that Renan would like to
have been, but mistrusts. He fulfills a heroic role, more specifically, in the context of the formation of Christianity: he is the
protagonist to whom the Church of Jerusalem plays the villain.
His great achievement is to have separated the child, the Christian Church, from her mother, Judaism. His great flaw, a source
of incalculable harm to the Christian cause, is the creation of
theology, which for Renan is a travesty of human reason. To him
must be traced the blame for the invention of the dogma of
original sin. And yet, he is somehow both narrow and "broad of
spirit" (*large d'esprit*), rigid and flexible, fanatical and willing
to make concessions.[10]

Although Renan begrudgingly respects this great figure, and
devotes to him some of the most moving pages of his entire
work, he must also judge him, like all the disciples, in the light
of Jesus; and here the portrait is at its harshest. At strategic intervals in the *Origines,* the "Galilean reality" is evoked and compared to what the Christian Church has become. Paul's immensely influential teachings were based not on the reality of
Jesus but on his *idea of Jesus.* A simple criterion guided Renan
in his testing of Christian works: "How much they contain of
Jesus." He is far from the scandalous simplicity of Nietzsche's
"the last Christian died on the cross." To grasp his view of the
matter, one must accept, and allow to exist side by side, what
seem to be two contradictory facts: the Christian Church derived from Jesus and yet distorted the image of Jesus. No total
break with Jesus ever occurred; there was always some continuity; the light of Jesus' spirit shone, however feebly, amid
the errors and illusions and pettinesses of his disciples. In a very
real sense the Church created Jesus after having been created
by him: *Jésus avait créé l'Eglise, l'Eglise le créait à son tour.*
And this creative process arose not from the work of two or
three "imposters," as so many naive eighteenth-century rationalists liked to believe, but spontaneously and understandably, in
"secret concert," from the very "entrails of humanity."

IV *Anti-Christ and Gospels*

From the relative unity of *Saint Paul* Renan returns, in *L'Anté-christ* (1873), to the more complex arrangement of triple themes we first noted in *Les Apôtres:* Christianity, Rome, Judea. He attaches great weight, in the solidification of Christianity, to the "epic" of the Roman amphitheater as expressed by the martyrs under Diocletian and Nero. The cruel festivities in Nero's gardens (August, 64 A.D.) he considers, after Golgotha itself, the second most solemn day in Christian history, establishing Rome as the symbolic and sacramental city of Christianity. Renan's Nero is interesting, among other reasons, for the fact that he is viewed not merely as the Anti-Christ, as created by the "last great prophet" in the "book of Nero" (the *Apocalypse*), but also in himself, as essentially a mediocre artist, miscast in the role of man of action. Nero's madness, Renan tells us with obvious ironic delight, is literary in origin; his most original discovery is that of the esthetics of martyrdom, of the *volupté de la pudeur.* Venus risks being dethroned by the beauty of the martyred Christian virgins. At times Renan comes close to assuming Nero's point of view, as he does for the Romans besieging Jerusalem. His stress on the exasperating fanaticism of the Jews, at one point, might incline the reader to suspect him of anti-Semitism, except that Jerusalem will exact her "revenge" by the eventual triumph over Rome of her offspring, Christianity.

L'Antéchrist is the first volume of the *Origines* written in the wake of the Franco-Prussian War; it betrays constant signs of Renan's sense of crisis and disillusionment. Its style is vigorously colloquial, spiced with irreverent wit, as though for the first time the historian were writing with shirt sleeves rolled up. The crises of Christianity, of Neronian Rome, of Judea, are made to reflect Renan's personal crisis at fifty, a *crise de dépression* in the midst of what is, basically, and what will once again resume being, an affirmative historical work. This is the volume in which Renan least resists the temptation to personal digression, as in the daydream recasting the dying Saint Paul as a skeptic, who would have merited our respect all the more had he been capable of practicing virtue without faith, of blending doubt and hope. It is also the volume in which the deliberate anachronism, so characteristic of the later books, begins to recur with ever greater frequency. The comparison of Nero to a bourgeois playing a monstrous role in some melodrama by Victor Hugo, is a striking example. Even more so is the comparison of the siege

of Jerusalem in the year 70 A.D. to the siege of Paris in 1871—a
rapprochement leading into one of Renan's favorite themes, the
risk a great nation must run of sacrificing its nationhood to its
more important role as a universal teacher of humanity.

In *Les Evangiles et la seconde génération chrétienne* (1877)
the key chapter (Chapter V) is significantly entitled, "The Fixa-
tion of the Legend and Teachings of Jesus." The Synoptic
Gospels represent for Renan "the masterpiece of spontaneous art
... sketched by an unconscious genius," and conferring a universal vogue upon the ancient Hebrew form of the *agada,* or
parable. The greatness of this form lies in its very *indécision,*
its lack of sharp contours; its beauty and power are in no way
vitiated by the almost total lack of "objective truth." After the
somber themes of *L'Antéchrist,* after Saint Paul, more concerned
with Jesus' death than with his life, and guilty of causing Christian theology to deviate from "the primitive evangelical ideal,"
Renan is pleased to find himself again, as in *Vie de Jésus,* in this
world of the Gospels, "the truly divine part of Christianity."
That is, Matthew and Mark; he is harsh on Luke, "the first
historian of Christianity," but a historian bent on history *ad
probandum* (providing legends to support dogmas) rather than
history *ad narrandum,* and therefore the first of the "ecclesiastical
historians." As for the Fourth Gospel, it is a pious fraud, though,
apart from the discourses attributed to Jesus, not entirely lacking
in historical value; it is the work not of John the Evangelist but
of his disciples. Renan makes little effort to conceal his distaste
for a work that tends to deny his own thesis of the essential
"Jewishness" of Christianity.

V *Christianity Fully Formed and a Rival Gospel*

We are, in *L'Eglise chrétienne* (1879), approaching the end
of the creative age of origins and the last stage in the "embryogeny" of Christianity. This waning age coincides with a century of rule by the most enlightened leaders the human race,
in Renan's opinion, has ever had: Hadrian, Antoninus, Marcus
Aurelius. The admirable fertility in the creation of legend dis-
played by the Gospels has exhausted itself. A final legend remains to be fixed, that of the reconciliation of Peter (conservatism) and Paul (revolution). The "instinctive labor" (*le
travail instinctif*), by means of which their apparently contradictory positions are reconciled, is comparable, and second in
importance only, to the creation of the legend of Jesus.

The last book of the *Origines, Marc-Aurèle et la fin du monde antique* (1882), is in many ways the finest. The *tableau parallèle* of pagan and Judeo-Christian worlds is at its most skilfully drawn; the "orchestration" of thematic materials at its most impressive, as is the unique Renanian blend of respect and irony toward his subject matter.[11] In a sense, the circle has come full round: in the first book Renan began by recreating the Gospel of Jesus, and in the last, he presents a rival Gospel, that of Marcus Aurelius's *Meditations*, "the Gospel of those who do not believe in the supernatural." Marcus Aurelius is the model— almost, but not quite, without defects—of the virtuous skeptic whose martyrdom (the "inner martyrdom" of the good man whose loved ones prove unworthy of him) is no less real, no less admirable, than those of Jesus or his disciples. Obviously the book is based on the opposition between Roman philosophy and Christian religion. Not only the purely natural piety of the Emperor but also the "good sense" of such critics of Christianity as Celsus and Lucian find great favor in Renan's eyes.

But one must not oversimplify. A great virtue of Renan the historian is his ability to assume the divergent points of view of all the actors in his story. *Le bon sens* is indeed a key phrase in the book. Yet the whole point is that Renan applies it *both* to Roman critics of Christianity and to the orthodox bishops who succeeded in maintaining, against all kinds of extremist heresies burgeoning around them, what they believed to be the traditions of primitive Christianity. Christianity is defined as "the relative good sense (*le bon sens relatif*) of the second century." The episcopacy plays a role in this book only a little less admirable than that of Marcus Aurelius. Although there is certainly irony in Renan's remark, "Mediocrity founded authority. Catholicism begins" (*La médiocrité fonda l'autorité. Le catholicisme commence*), the bishops clinging to orthodoxy emerge as far more positive figures than the heretical Gnostics and Montanists, with their abortive attempts to make an aristocracy out of the Church, the former by exaggerating the importance of rational knowledge, the latter by wishing to exclude sinners.

Renan finds the basic ecclesiastical structure of Christianity, as well as its basic doctrines and at least the *germes* of the sacraments, established by the year 180. The child has fully detached itself from its mother, Judaism, and is in full possession of all its faculties. The history of origins is concluded and "ecclesiastical history" begins. Briefly, Renan depicts the eventual changes (*les transformations ultérieures*) which the Christian religion will undergo in later centuries. It is a bleak picture of superstition and idolatry, of embellishments (*fioritures*) removing the Christian faith further than ever from the Gospels, until it becomes "an edition of Judaism adapted to Indo-European taste" (*une édition du judaïsme accommodée au goût indo-européen*). The concluding pages, forming a kind of epilogue, are less history than a prognosis of Christianity's future, a stock-taking, or *bilan*, of its chances for survival. For all his protestations of not wishing to convert anyone to anything, Renan is not sparing in his suggestions as to how Catholicism, in particular, might come to terms with the modern world if it hopes to survive as something more than a magnificent ruin. Unfortunately, from a Catholic point of view, his blueprint for the "Church in the Modern World" calls for excisions of supernaturalism which no ecumenical council could be expected to agree with.

VI   Return to Israel: The Origins of Christian Origins

Israel, by virtue of Renan's thesis that Christianity was a *fait primitivement juif*, is never lost sight of completely in *Les Origines du christianisme*. Upon finishing this work, in the full maturity of his powers, he turned, or more precisely returned, to the detailed demonstration of his thesis, in what we might call "the origins of Christian origins." In the course of an affectionate tribute to a modern Jew whom he admired, his publisher, Calmann-Lévy, who had just died, Renan describes the *Histoire du peuple d'Israël* in the following metaphorical terms: "The arch of the bridge which remained for me to throw between Judaism and Christianity is now established. In the *Vie de Jésus*, I tried to show the majestic growth of the Galilean tree from the tip of its roots to its summit. . . . Now I believe I have succeeded in making known the sub-soil where the roots of Jesus grew (*le sous-sol où poussèrent les racines de Jésus.*)" Thus Renan closed "the cycle of religious history which I have embraced as my life's task."

Despite the immense size of *Histoire du peuple d'Israël*, the author's inspiration flags remarkably little. Like a modern Antæus he seems to have regained strength from touching the ground of Jewish history. There are dull stretches, what the French call *longueurs* (the endless dates and successions of rulers, etc.). But the result is on the whole as readable as *Les Origines*. Renan's power of construction is certainly one reason for this readability: his adroitness in keeping the major themes before us, his sense of the *grandes masses* of his tableaux, his use of such devices as pauses to recapitulate (*haltes* or *points d'arrêts*), foreshadowings, and codas. The artistic sense he brought to the writing of history has in no way diminished.

In the obscure beginnings of the Jewish people, when "tales of the marvelous" abound and historical reality is hard to extract from them, a deliberate dryness in his style offsets all the more effectively the legendary quality of the material he must interpret. (Compare Voltaire's delighted horror in cataloguing Old Testament immoralities, as though each barbaric act were a recorded fact.) A sense of movement and progression carries the reader along to what is the climax of the work: the solemn hour (the year is 536 B.C.) in which the Jewish conscience reached the highest and clearest point of its vision, in the "great anonymous prophet" (Isaiah), and the juncture is accomplished between, on the one hand, the patriarchal religion of the past, and, on the other, the evangelical religion of Jesus. At this point, "Iahvé [Jehovah] has become once again and completely the Elohim of the patriarchs." For, "the anonymous prophet of 536 is the culmination of three centuries of the greatest religious effort (Christianity excepted) in human history. With him we are atop a mountain from which Jesus can be perceived on another distant summit, and in between, a very great depression." If the last few hundred pages after this climactic point give the effect of a falling away (*déchéance*), of a great sleep (*un grand sommeil*), these "troughs" and phases of decadence are in the story itself as the historian conceives it; he may perhaps be pardoned for faithfully imitating them in his presentation. In any case, throughout the work Renan makes generous use of Old Testament texts to support his argument, and these (especially the Psalms, translated with great poetic skill) have the effect, when the reader begins to feel the massive tale weigh a bit heavily upon him, of refreshing his spirit.

According to Renan's helpful custom of announcing, in the preface of one book, the leading idea to be found in the book immediately following, he has provided us (Preface to *Marc-Aurèle*) with the best possible summary of the *Histoire du peuple d'Israël*. He writes:

Christianity begins in the eighth century before Christ, when the great prophets, seizing hold of the people of Israel, make of them the people of God, charged with inaugurating in the world a purified cult (*le culte pur*). Until then, the religion of Israel had not differed essentially from the self-centered and selfish cult which was that of all neighboring tribes and which is revealed to us, for example, by the inscription of King Mésa. A revolution took place when an inspired prophet, not belonging to the priesthood, dared to say: "Can you believe that God takes pleasure in the smoke of your victims, in the fat of your rams? Abandon these sacrifices which sicken him, and do good." Isaiah is in this sense the first founder of Christianity. Jesus really did no more than repeat, in a charming and popular language, what had been said seven hundred and fifty years before him in classical Hebrew.

The aim of these ten final books of Renan's Judeo-Christian cycle is "to show how the religion of Israel, which originally had no superiority over the cults of Ammon or Moab, became a real religion, and how the religious history of the Jewish people was marked by a constant progress toward worship in spirit and in truth (*le culte en esprit et en vérité*)."

Within this broad structural framework three main interlocking themes (not to mention countless lesser motifs) may be discerned, like the musical themes of a Wagnerian drama. First, the struggle of the idea of a patriarchal God (Elohism) with the idea of a local or nationalistic God (Jahvehism), ending in the final triumph of Elohism, restored, renewed, heightened by the Prophets in the form of the universalized and predominantly ethical religion of monotheism, with a minimum of dogma, ritual and supernaturalism. The second theme is that of the "Jewish miracle" (*le miracle juif*). The truly great contribution of Israel, for Renan, is its *messianisme*, or belief in the attainment of *justice on earth*. This is, in his opinion, the stem from which all subsequent movements of social reform have grown, or upon which they have been grafted, from Christianity itself, destined to carry this part of the Jewish message to the whole of humanity, down to nineteenth-century socialism. (Renan would certainly have included Marx as a descendant of the Prophets, had he had occasion to mention his work.)

The need to believe in an afterworld was not originally part of this messianic ideal, and developed later as a way out of the dilemma (dramatized in the *Book of Job*) of the just man cruelly treated in this world while the unjust prosper. The *miracle juif* is contrasted with the *miracle grec*: the Jews have given us "socialism," the Greeks "liberalism" (Renan uses these terms not in any narrow partisan, but in the broadest moral, sense). The Prophets have raised a cry of justice that can never again be

stifled; the Greeks have created the ideal of a free and rational
lay society, but with little concern for the sufferings of the weak.
"The world's movement," writes Renan, "is the result of the
parallelogram of two forces (*la résultante du parallélogramme
de deux forces*), liberalism, which is of Greek origin, and socialism, which is of Hebrew origin, liberalism tending toward the
maximum development of human nature, socialism taking account, above all, of justice in the strictest sense and of the
happiness of the greatest number, which is often sacrificed by
liberalism to the needs of civilization and of the state."

The great stress Renan lays on the social, as distinct from the
political, strength of the "Jewish miracle" gives rise to his third
theme: the sacrifice a people may be called upon to make of its
political power, in fact of its very existence as a nation, in order
to carry out a more universal spiritual or religious mission. He
never tired of savoring the irony of the Jewish lesson or of suggesting that it might have relevance for the modern age of
nationalist cults:

> The thinkers of Israel are the first to revolt against the injustices of
> the world, to refuse to bow to those inequalities, abuses, and privileges
> without which there can be neither an army nor a strong society. . . .
> All sensible people of Jerusalem toward the year 500 B.C. were furious
> with the prophets who rendered impossible all military and diplomatic
> action. But what a pity if these sublime madmen had been stopped!
> Jerusalem would have gained by being a bit longer the capital of an
> insignificant kingdom; she would never have become the religious
> capital of humanity.

VII *History as Comedy*

Every historian who hopes to give us more than what Lytton
Strachey called "a large heap of sawdust" must write from a distinct point of view. At the heart of Renan's "historical system"
(to use his own phrase) is the concept of history as "comedy."
The term as I think he understood it needs to be very carefully
defined. The key text for doing so is to be found in *Histoire du
peuple d'Israël,* in the chapter entitled "David, King of Jerusalem" (Book II, Chapter XVIII), more precisely, in the last
paragraph of what is the concluding chapter of this book. Renan
finds it highly amusing, even "comic" in the simplest sense of
the word, that David, for him at best a mixture of good and evil,
"the brigand of Adullam and Siklag," should be transformed into

a saint, the author of the Psalms, the leader of the sacred chorus
(*le chorège sacré*), the prototype of the future Saviour. "Jesus
will be the son of David!" he exclaims. "Pious souls will forever
believe that they are in communion with this bandit; humanity
will believe in ultimate justice on the testimony of David, who
never gave it a thought, and of the Sibyll, who never existed.
Teste David cum Sibylla! Oh divine comedy!"

Taken out of context, this apparent basing of Judeo-Christian
hopes on error and illusion seems to partake of the type of devastating anti-religious wit one finds in Voltaire, Mencken, or Ber-
trand Russell. Replaced in the great context of Renan's historical
work, it has a far different meaning. For the whole tenor and
movement of that work tend to establish clearly that Renan himself shared the belief of Jews and Christians—though not their
reasons for believing—that mankind is evolving toward truth
and justice. It is in this sense—the sense of a dramatic work
progressing, despite vicissitudes that are often cruel or ridiculous,
toward a "happy ending"—that he compares history to a comedy.
The historical tradition to which he belongs, for all his greater
skepticism and positivism, is that of Bossuet and Michelet, the
tradition of history with a purpose and an end. But whereas the
first viewed history as a sermon in the noble style on the theme
of Providence, and the second, as a sublime but purely human
melodrama with distinct heroes and villains, Renan views it, in
his essay on the historian Augustin Thierry, as a "comedy at once
divine and human." [12]

In what sense, "divine"? By now we know Renan too well to
expect him to mean that a personal God intervenes in human
affairs or guides them providentially. His *divin*, as we have seen
in *L'Avenir de la science*, is the spiritual potential of mankind
itself. Renan is above all the historian of the idea, the ideal, the
spirit. He has no interest in rendering the wealth of concrete and
colorful detail—what people wore, ate, how they smelled—that
one finds in Romantic historians, such as his mentor, Augustin
Thierry, or Michelet, that *totalité des mœurs* which Taine admired in Flaubert's historical tale *Hérodias*. One never finds in
his historical work a sentence such as this from Flaubert's
description of a banquet in ancient Judea: "They served bull
kidneys, dormice, nightingales, and minced meat in vine leaves;
while the priests discussed the question of resurrection." But he
is interested in the idea of resurrection, how it originated, what
portion of truth there may be in it. The "divine comedy" of

history means the eventual triumph of the ideal as he conceived it, and this inevitable, almost logical dénouement is what prevents history from being, for him, either tragic or meaningless. His indebtedness to Hegel for this concept is undeniable; like Hegel, he is a philosopher of history, though he is also more of a pure historian.[13] His originality lies in working out this concept in terms of the concrete unfolding of Judeo-Christian beliefs, with their two embodiments of the religious ideal, Isaiah and Jesus, "who is already contained entire in Isaiah."

The chief reason that Renan is less disgusted than Voltaire by the seamier side of Judeo-Christian history—apart from the fact that he had a better sense than Voltaire of what may have been merely legend or exaggeration, and no need whatever to discredit either Judaism or Christianity—is that he judges not the documents in themselves, as testimonies to human weakness or baseness, but their role as instruments in the working out of a higher human purpose. In other words, nothing in what he calls the "somber grand opera" of the Old Testament, or in its moments of low comedy, can diminish the vision of Isaiah, nor can the foibles and innocent self-deceptions of Jesus' disciples reduce his stature. Humanity is at times a "stupid species" (*une sotte espèce*), more often it is *la pauvre humanité*, but its unfailing advantage is the immense time span in which its life unfolds and in which its "unconscious reason" or god-like potential works out its purposes. In the light of this *raison inconsciente*, history is a void from which a "parcel of justice and truth" is being drawn; even *folies* and *excès* contribute to progress; they are in any case inseparable from it. Thus we read in *Histoire du peuple d'Israël* (VI, pp. 1156 and 1222): "Through absurdities that wear themselves out, poor reason, which allows nothing to be wasted, continually advances. . . . The absurdity of the detail must not mask the grandeur of the work as a whole" (*L'absurdité du détail ne doit pas masquer la grandeur de l'œuvre*).[14]

When Marcel Proust tried to assimilate Renan's historical work to an Offenbach operetta and ridiculed it as *la belle Hélène du christianisme*, he was, ironically, closer to the truth than he realized. He *almost* saw the point of the Renanian comedy of history; but misled by what looked like touches of frivolity, of mere Second Empire gaiety, he failed to grasp the true coloration of the work, derived from the calmly optimistic view of history as inevitably dual in nature, a blend of realism and idealism. "Human things," observes Renan, "are composed of matter and spirit. Freedom and servitude, that which pushes man forward and that which holds him back, the sublime and the *terre-à-terre*, are equally necessary to construct a great ensemble which lives."

VIII   *The Historian Judged*

Renan the historian has often been criticized for the wrong reasons. In the first place, he is hardly so "subjective" as some of his critics have made him out to be. His Ecclesiastes and Jesus, Paul and Nero and Marcus Aurelius all bear some resemblance to himself, to be sure, but they nevertheless exist as objects of independent study. He is not weak in or indifferent to documentation. (The so-called "popular" edition of the *Vie de Jésus*, without footnotes or references, may have led to this misunderstanding.) On the contrary, he vigorously upholds and consistently practices, the theory of historical writing as *both art and science*. (Every apprentice historian should ponder his well-balanced and profound description of the historical craft, in "M. Augustin Thierry," *Essais de morale et de critique*). He is not nearly so skeptical as he is alleged to be. In fact the Protestant critics of his day, Edmond Schérer in particular, were much closer to the truth in charging him with insufficient skepticism toward his Biblical sources. Viewed in retrospect today, and especially as compared with the more rigorous and systematic skepticism of German rationalists, such as Strauss, Renan's interpretation of Christianity as a historical religion founded by a historical Jesus and in full possession of its essential doctrines and structure by the end of the second century, has, ironically enough, much to commend it to the most orthodox Catholic historiographers.

A fairer appraisal of his greatness as a historian may be obtained by frankly admitting his true weaknesses as inseparable from his true strengths. In other words, as with most writers of well-defined genius, he had the defects of his qualities. It was a distinct merit on his part, to begin with, not to limit himself to the relating of only what can be known (or at least presumed to be known) with certainty "to have happened." To this narrowly positivistic method, of which the German historian Ranke is the most famous exemplar, he wisely refused to subscribe. In theory his ideal would have been to indicate the "certain," the "probable," the "plausible," and the "possible," typographically, by the use of inks of different colors.[15] In practice a generous recourse to the adverb "perhaps" (*peut-être*) allows him to distinguish between what can be established with reasonable certainty and what "might have happened" (*ce qui a pu arriver*). Yet if he gained by rejecting what has now become an outmoded rigorism and by making intelligent use of what a contemporary American historian of Christianity calls "probable guesses," [16] he also at times abuses the right to hypothesis. Can the reconstruction of the past, the reader asks himself, be this neat, this satisfying to the esthetic sense? Can history have been this purposeful?

Similarly double-edged—both defect and quality—is Renan's famous use of the anachronism, more precisely his use of modern terms to characterize ancient personages or events: the Prophets as the first *journalistes,* the siege of Jerusalem in terms of the siege of Paris, Jesus as socialist or anarchist, Nero as a Romantic, etc. Strictly speaking, these are not "anachronisms," since he is generally very attentive to the nature of historical phenomena as unique and unrepeatable events; he is also very attentive to chronology, as the reader will see merely by glancing at the majority of his pages, which are headed by precise dates. Furthermore, he defends quite convincingly (for he was sensitive to criticism on this score) his "rapprochements between ancient events . . . and movements of modern times," especially his insistence on Jewish history as the best example of "the opposition between political questions and social questions" (see Preface to Books V-VI, *Histoire du peuple d'Israël*). There is no doubt that such rapprochements lend great vitality to his work.[17] Yet they take him at times—it is a fact of piquant irony—far from that *historia ad narrandum* that he claimed was the merit of his century, to the very *historia ad probandum* that he saw as the defect (though a beguiling one) of Christian historians, beginning with the Gospels! To a far greater extent than he may have been aware, Renan has written a new Gospel, the Gospel of humanity.[18] At times, one has the uneasy feeling of being confronted not with history, but with an analysis of contemporary themes set against an ancient backdrop. How, for example, would Renan have treated the destruction of Jerusalem if he had written of it *before* the siege of Paris?

Every historian is to some extent a student of origins, attempting to explain how things have grown from their beginnings to become what they are today. Renan's error—the error of much historical writing in the nineteenth century—is known as the "genetic fallacy," or the illusory belief that by the mere fact of revealing beginnings one reveals "causes," that by explaining origins one has *sufficiently* explained all. The great modern French historian, Marc Bloch, has reproached Renan and his contemporaries for this obsession with origins, which became with them a cult. "The oak is born from the acorn," Bloch agrees. "But oak it becomes and remains only if it meets with favorable conditions of milieu, conditions which have nothing to do with embryology" (*Apologie pour l'histoire*, p. 7). The "demon of judgment," as Bloch calls it, usually presides over the cult of origins, for the historical geneticists almost invariably believe also that the origins of a belief or other phenomenon are somehow purer, more pristine, than the same belief fully developed or continuing to grow. Thus, Renan despises Christian history after Marcus Aurelius as a falling away, a petering out of inspiration, and with a wave of his hand dismisses it as mere *histoire ecclé-siastique*, inferior in interest to the earlier, supposedly more creative periods. According to this logic, the greatness of a Luther or a Wesley, a Newman or a John XXIII becomes impossible.

Yet, *felix culpa*, one is tempted to say. "Geneticism" provided Renan with superb technical advantages. Few historians have had his success in arranging comparable masses of material in such a well-unified whole, or in conferring upon this whole such a distinct sense of movement and growth, or of what H. Stuart Hughes calls "the direction of change through time."

IX *A Pretext for Saying Everything*

Periodically, especially in the last half-century, historians have urged that history be written by the "whole man" rather than by the mere specialist, and for educated readers rather than for other specialists. The goal of the *Annales d'histoire économique et sociale*, of which Bloch was a co-founder, is to try "to explain the world to cultivated minds, in the light of historical method." With all his faults Renan possesses undeniably the virtue—and without reservations this time—of writing as a "whole man" for the widest possible audience, yet with a minimum of sacrifice to his standards and discipline as a scholar. In Renan as historian, the artist and philosopher, the moral, religious, and political thinker, each has a voice. Thoughts of past, present, and future all form part of a long, richly varied, marvelously subtle meditation on the human condition.[19] History was for him the great achievement of his century, and its greatness lay in its being a "pretext for saying everything," *un prétexte à tout dire* ("M. Augustin Thierry"). It was for him what tragedy or epic had been for the classical writer, what *philosophie* had been for the eighteenth century, the *drame* for the Romantics, or what the novel has been in the last hundred years. Because of the breadth and profundity he conferred on the historical art, we can the more easily forgive the actual narrowness of his vision: his equating the "human spirit" so obsessively with the *miracle juif* or the *miracle grec*, his blindness to Oriental cultures, as though one could claim to speak of "humanity" while virtually ignoring, for example, the Chinese peoples who make up a fourth of the human race.

Here at last, in history, was the *œuvre de synthèse* he had been seeking since his critical years in the seminary. Despite passing temptations to doubt the validity of history as a science, he never lost his belief in it, his zeal for it. Had he lived longer, he tells us in the Preface of his last book, the *Feuilles détachées*, he would have had "projects enough for three or four lives" and been eager to undertake them—a history of the French Revolution, a history of Athens, a history of science and free thought, a history of Brittany "in six volumes." He would even—finally!—have learned Chinese and turned to the study of Chinese civilization. Surely, such an example cannot have wholly lost its power to stimulate young would-be historians, young students of literature and thought in general. Nor can the reader who is willing to brush aside preconceived ideas of what Renan is supposed to be, and to read his historical work with unbiased eyes, fail to be impressed by the strength it takes from his own vivid presence in its pages. The origins of Christianity are also a meditation on the origins of Renan. Each one of us, as he puts it, is our "historical system"; each one of us is haunted by his origins (*On est toujours hanté par ses origines*). The vitality his work preserves is largely due to the force underlying it of a personal search for the rational understanding of a faith ("history" means, etymologically, "inquiry"), a personal effort to transpose that faith meaningfully, though de-supernaturalized, into the modern world, by discovering the adaptability of its messianic drive to men of a post-Christian age. Like so much great history, it has the vigor of a re-enactment, and thus once again, the nature of a "comedy" in its original sense of a "play." The clue with which it provides us to the unity of Renan's thought is that he aspired to play both Jesus and Marcus Aurelius, both Isaiah and Ecclesiastes.

Had Renan written nothing more than *Les Origines du christianisme* and *Histoire du peuple d'Israël*, he would rank very high among French authors. Yet such was the breadth of his genius—his *grande envergure*, as the French would call it, a term borrowed from nautical vocabulary and describing the powerful spread of a great sail in the wind—that his gift for history, though permeating all his other talents, does not fully explain or exhaust them. His critical intelligence, his artistic imagination, hold in store still other forms of expression that can lay claim to greatness.

CHAPTER 6

A Critic of the French State

U NIVERSAL criticism" was singled out by Renan in *L'Avenir de la science*, it will be remembered, as the distinguishing feature of nineteenth-century thought. The "critic," ideally, proceeds independently of established traditions, without preconceived views, hesitantly, anxious not to lose any aspect of the infinite variety of things or to oversimplify their infinite complexity. The "moralist," on the other hand, is aware of and concerned to preserve certain values transmitted to him by past generations; he judges more trenchantly, affirms more readily "what he believes to be the best"; he is guided by "an essentially conservative instinct for beautiful and good things," *cet instinct essentiellement conservateur des belles et bonnes choses*. (For these distinctions between *critique and moraliste*, see "M. de Sacy et l'Ecole libérale," *Essais de morale et de critique*.) The questioning, detached, sometimes radical critic coexists in Renan with the conservative moralist—one reason for the originality and fascination of his work. But he is also, much more vigorously and markedly than he has been recognized to be, the reformer, the lay preacher, diagnosing the ills of his time, prescribing remedies. The fervor with which he is capable of denouncing the errors of his age—some of which are still the errors of our age— and recalling it to the path of reason and perfection makes of him, in fact, a prophet. It would have been surprising if in his long, intimate association with the Hebrew prophets, as a historian, some of their zeal had not rubbed off upon him.

As critic, moralist, and prophet, Renan confronted almost all the great issues of his day: moral, intellectual, religious, educational, political. (I say "almost," because only economic and social issues are neglected by him.) The individual and the state; the meaning of freedom and liberalism; revolution and tradition; authoritarian versus popular rule; the situation of Catholicism and of higher education in France; an assessment of the "French mind" (*l'esprit français*); France and Germany; nationalism and internationalism—to these questions, which have lost little of

85

their relevance today, he returned again and again. In scores of
articles and public addresses, beginning in 1848 with his contributions to the republican journal, *La Liberté de penser*, and
down to his last speeches, a year or so before his death, he established himself as a prolific interpreter and judge of his age, an
intellectual and moral "voice" or "conscience" comparable to
Camus or Sartre in modern France. From time to time he gathered articles and speeches into books, of which I propose to discuss four in this chapter: *Essais de morale et de critique* (1859),
Questions contemporaines (1868), *La Réforme intellectuelle et
morale* (1871), and *Discours et conférences* (1887).[1]

I Moral Resistance

The major theme of *Essais de morale et de critique*, announced
in the Preface, is the definition of "the essential task of our time,
that of establishing liberty through the regeneration of the individual conscience" (*la fondation de la liberté par la régénéra-
tion de la conscience individuelle*). This theme is elaborated upon
in a series of meditative essays, full of poetic touches, designed
to illustrate means by which the individual conscience can resist
succumbing to false concepts of freedom and to a relatively new
and more dangerous—because more subtle and more pervasive—
form of tyranny. Although the book appeared during the seventh
year of the authoritarian Second Empire, its villain is not so
much Napoleon III as the type of centralized and monstrously
expanding bureaucratic state, admired of monarchists, republicans, and imperialists alike, which reduces the individual to the
role of a mere cog. The real evil against which its author protests
is the type of slavery, mistaken for freedom, into which he feared
the modern industrialized state was leading mankind, a *ma-
térialisme vulgaire* which would transform individual members
of society into (the metaphor is one of the most terrifying in all
Renan) "a vast field of corn all of whose stalks bend in unison
at the slightest gust of wind" (*un vaste champ d'épis dont un
coup de vent fait fléchir à la fois toutes les têtes*). The surrender,
so gradual as to be almost imperceptible, of traditional rights
and freedoms to the state, in return for material comforts and
the guarantee of "equality," the slow degeneration of the individual conscience to the point of "degrading do-nothingness and
resigned inertia"—this is the diabolical drift of things against
which Renan resists. His vision of it is remarkably close to
twentieth-century societies of mass men and contented robots, in

whatever parts of the so-called "free" or "unfree" worlds they may happen to flourish.

To counteract this encroachment upon individual rights by the *raison d'Etat,* this stifling of spiritual vitality by *l'esprit industriel et·utilitaire,* Renan calls for the formation of a spiritual élite, in his words an *imperceptible aristocratie,* capable of regenerating in modern society something of the moral sensitiveness, the idealism, the poetic spirit associated, in pre-revolutionary France, with aristocracies of class. These invisible aristocrats, he hoped, would constitute a spiritual state within the political state, a *cité idéale* or *église d'élite* radiating outward and revitalizing a society benumbed by "vulgarity" and "mediocrity."

Renan's program of reform consists essentially of setting up against the materialism of his age various examples of spirituality drawn from the recent and more remote European past, including the Romantic era, the seventeenth century, the Middle Ages, and the golden age of the "Celtic races." At first glance, his book seems like a simple collection of essays dealing with various historical subjects, each essay using a work under review as the pretext for original reflections. On closer reading, each historical subject assumes, within the context of the book's regenerative purpose, a symbolic value, and the book itself becomes, in effect, a kind of repertory or mosaic of symbols.

II *Negative and Positive Symbols*

Three of the symbols are wholly or almost wholly negative. The fifteenth-century *Farce de Maître Patelin* represents the decline of the medieval *grand idéal aristocratique* and prefigures the advent of bourgeois materialism, anti-heroism, and chicanery. The Papacy, as manipulated by the Roman Curia, betokens the degeneration of a once "universal Church" into an instrument of Italian nationalism, powerless to effect meaningful religious reform. The Exposition Universelle in Paris (1855), a prototype of the World's Fair, displaying the wares of modern culture (see the essay ironically entitled "La Poésie de l'Exposition"), confirms Renan's fear that his century was moving "neither toward good nor toward evil, but toward mediocrity." [2]

Four themes carry symbolic meaning that is partly negative and partly positive. The history of revolutions in Italy, though riddled with corruption and decadence, is admirable for the virility of its political energy (an interpretation which resembles Stendhal's). Renan reserves special admiration for the revolu-

tionary Benedictine monk, Dom Luigi Tosti, whose rational mysticism and whose concept of history as the "Gospel of humanity"
(a high point of which is the Italian struggle for national uni-
fication and freedom) left a deep impression upon him. The
Italian sense of zealous commitment to a political cause Renan
contrasts with the apathy of his fellow citizens in France of the
Second Empire. With all her evils, Italy has at least managed to
escape sinking to "the fatal level of modern banality" (*le fatal
niveau de la banalité moderne*). "If the ideal of a nation," writes
Renan, "is to reach that excess of timidity where every diversity
of opinion is forestalled by administrative measures and that
degree of uniformity where the pitch of the street-organs (*les
orgues de Barbarie*) is regulated by the State, then a country
[Italy] where things differed sharply though separated by only
a few miles distance and where the freedom to hate was carried
to extreme limits must seem supremely barbaric" ("Les Révolu-
tions d'Italie"). For three of his French contemporaries belonging to the Romantic generation whose positive legacy he is
anxious to preserve, that is, Sacy, Cousin, and Lamennais, Renan
has similarly qualified praise: he disentangles their merits and
defects with all the deftness of a brilliant surgeon. All three,
writers active in public affairs, *philosophes doublés d'artistes* like
himself, clearly belong to a spiritual aristocracy. Yet Sacy and
Cousin betray the weakness of that *libéralisme* which Renan had
come to view as part of the "heavy legacy of the French Revolution," and whose most dangerous error was to believe that
individual rights and freedoms are best guaranteed by more and
more "administration." As for the great defrocked priest and
apostate, Lamennais, he symbolizes the futility of trying to reconcile Catholicism and Revolution, the impossibility of "liberaliz-
ing" the Catholic Church from within; yet to his failure Renan
wisely grants a touch of tragic nobility.

Four essay subjects, finally, seem to convey an almost wholly
positive symbolism. The French Academy is endowed by Renan
with a social and moral, and perhaps also a political, significance
far transcending its literary origins in the seventeenth century.
It becomes the model of the quasi-autonomous association needed
to counteract both the tyranny of the state and the tyranny of a
mauvais goût which threatens to destroy the traditional *délicatesse de l'esprit français*. The second and third such positive
symbols are two historians, a Frenchman and a German, whose
examples had profoundly influenced Renan himself. To Augustin

Thierry he paid one of the most moving tributes with which one historian has honored another, using the occasion also to give us what must rank among the wisest essays ever written on the art and science of historiography. Within the symbolic framework of the *Essais de morale et de critique,* Thierry represents another type of antidote to political apathy, more specifically the apathy of historians who would resign themselves to the "fate" of their times, renounce all hope of shaping political events, and retreat into ivory towers of antiquarianism. The guiding principle of Thierry's genius—it is also a major component of Renan's own greatness—is the conviction that "the wide sense of human things [necessary to the historian] is obtained only by the understanding of the present, and the present gives up its secret only in proportion to the stake (*l'enjeu*) one has in it." The essay on the German historian of Greek religions, Friedrich Creuzer, brings a touch of humor and whimsicality about two thirds of the way through a book that is on the whole not especially playful (the word *sérieux* occurs in it with high frequency). But there can be no doubt about the seriousness of the lesson taught by this product of a heroic age of German scholarship, when erudition was allied with the sense of philosophy and religion: here is a corrective to the French tendency to equate learning with pedantry, religion with dogma, and philosophy with abstract reasoning divorced from "the knowledge of facts and of history."

The fourth and supreme symbol of spiritual resistance is described in the last, and longest, essay in the book, "La Poésie des races celtiques," which, as Renan points out in his preface, "explains" all those that have preceded it. As a Breton, and therefore a Celt, Renan was eager to introduce to his readers the very great poetic heritage, seminal in the formation of European literatures, of the Celtic peoples (the word "races" has here an ethnic rather than a strictly biological sense). His essay is, in the first place, then, a masterpiece of *haute vulgarisation,* or scholarship rendered accessible to a wide public. He was also eager to repay a debt to his own spiritual ancestors, who had taught him among other lessons that life is not merely "a personal adventure that each one runs on his own account and at his own risks," but "a link in a long tradition, a gift received and transmitted, a debt paid and a duty accomplished." This idea is central to the enlightened traditionalism of the whole book. A note of personal piety, therefore, foreshadowed in the apostrophe to the Celtic saints with which the book's preface concludes, informs and heightens the scholarly presentation. "The old memories of this race are more for me than a curious subject of study; this is the region where my imagination has always been happy to wander, and where I love to seek refuge as in an ideal fatherland (*où j'aime à me réfugier comme dans une idéale patrie*).

But most important of all, Renan's idealized Celt (there are both history and idealization in his essay) is meant to be opposed to the barbarian of nineteenth-century France, and, more broadly speaking, to the barbarian of modern industrial society. The genuine *poésie des races celtiques* is juxtaposed and contrasted with the false *poésie de l'Exposition*. The essay is intended to have "an esthetic and moral value much more than a scholarly purpose"—another way, I think, of expressing the symbolic function which it shares with most of the other essays in the collection. The Celt signifies "powerful individuality" and resistance to a much more dangerous invasion than that of enemy tribes fought off in the past: the invasion of "modern civilization, so destructive of regional varieties and national types." The Celtic example is a kind of leaven to raise the spiritual quality of modern life, a salt to restore its savor. Perhaps, Renan hopes, it is not too late for the Frenchman to unlearn the habits that make him a perfect citizen of the modern state—passivity, conformity, selfish preoccupation with material well being, tastelessness, platitudinous "good sense," with its accompanying indifference to poetry—and to learn from the "primitive" Celt the value of closeness to nature and to the "life hidden in nature," of openness to the quest of the "unknown," of a free and fanciful imagination, of stubborn individual integrity, of devotion to a cause that transcends one's ego, and of a life guided by idealistic vision, rather than aimlessly driven on by endless acquisitiveness of material possessions.

III　*Importunate Truths*

Between *Essais de morale et de critique* and the two books published, one toward the end of the Second Empire (*Questions contemporaines*) and the other after its collapse as a result of the Franco-Prussian War (*La Réforme intellectuelle et morale*), there is a great contrast. The first of these three works is esthetically the most satisfying. It was composed in such a way that each of its thirteen essays may stand alone, conveying its meaning independently, while each nevertheless gains by its setting in what is a skillfully constructed whole, a subtle fabric, having its own beauty. This achievement is all the more astonishing because the work is based on a collection of articles and such collections rarely make true "books." Renan recognized that the defense of idealism he had undertaken was too much a matter of "moral instinct" (*sentiment moral*), of values tested empirically by generations who have lived by them, to admit of rational or logical proof. He therefore put the strength of his "demonstration" in the cumulative impression made upon the reader by the rhythmic balance of his sentences, the force of a strategically placed image or a soberly lyrical passage, the concrete details of a moral portrait. This method, closer to poetry than to the common notion of journalism, he described as "grasping one's object by way of successive approximations" (*serrer son objet par des approximations successives*). Given this definition of his essay method, it comes as no surprise that he claimed critics and historians to have been "the true poets" of his time.

Questions contemporaines and *La Réforme intellectuelle et morale*, by contrast, attack contemporary issues, especially political issues, in a much more direct and forthright manner and in the kind of unornamented style which the French call *dépouillé*. Of the urgency of such issues, Renan had come to be more and more aware, to the point where he consented to run for the office of *député* to the National Assembly in 1869. The first book is sober, moderate, somewhat dry, with few touches of poetry. The second, composed largely of *écrits de circonstance*, written much closer to the turbulent events they seek to interpret, the fateful problems they seek to solve, is riddled with extremist proposals for the political reform of France, most of which, fortunately, Renan was willing to reconsider when he later returned to his more reflective self. *La Réforme intellectuelle et morale* is both unfailingly provocative—at times exasperatingly so—and illumined by flashes of apocalyptic imagery that seem to be in direct proportion to the "reactionary" nature of the ideas they express. No one who has read this work could possibly claim, as Gide did, that Renan's style is uniformly "soft," "uncertain," "flaccid," or "lacking in muscle,"[3] or, as so many of his foes have claimed, that he was incapable of taking an unequivocal stand on important issues.

Three major problematic areas of French life under the Second Empire are surveyed by Renan in the *Questions contemporaines:* politics, education, and the moral and religious state of France. The unifying theme is the meaning, conditions, and value of freedom, as applied to all three domains. A great part of the book is taken up with an attack on Catholic orthodoxy and a defense of the author's religious philosophy, for which he had been dismissed from his Chair of Hebrew at the Collège de France. Once again, Renan affirms that the essence of "science" as well as of a "purified religion" is to leave out of account the supernatural (*faire abstraction du surnaturel*) and that the true enemies of the religious spirit in France are Catholic orthodoxy and the revolutionary poet Béranger's *Dieu des bonnes gens* or God of the "man in the street"—two religions, one dogmatic and the other frivolous, between which he establishes curious and disturbing affinities.

Renan's views on education, as presented in this and other works, though important enough to merit much fuller treatment, will have to be very briefly summarized here. He found these main flaws in the French educational system: (1) neglect of scientific, mathematical, and historical studies in favor of literary studies (as serious an error, he believed, as claiming that these last should be the monopoly of the future *homme de lettres*); (2) sacrifice of solid knowledge and original thought to mere oratory and rhetoric, so that the Frenchman becomes, we might say, all form and no content; (3) too highly centralized a bureaucratic administration, with an exaggerated role assigned to the University of Paris; (4) too dominant and rigid control over education by the state (which has encroached even on "moral education" rightfully belonging to the family), resulting in a regimentation that threatens to reduce the pupil to an automaton. The correctness of Renan's assessment of these various defects and the wisdom of his proposals to remedy them are borne out by the official reforms begun in his own day (to some extent under his influence) and renewed in our own, for these reforms have been designed, in great part, to provide precisely the stronger scientific training, the greater intellectual substance and balance, and the granting of more autonomy to provincial universities, which he called for.

Politically, *Questions contemporaines*, like *Essais de morale et de critique*, belongs to the eighteenth-century liberal tradition of "checks and balances." Its author rejects the concept of an all-powerful state charged with administering freedom and justice according to abstract, a priori principles (a concept he blames on Rousseau and the French Revolution), in favor of a kind of political laissez-faire, according to which centralized power is checked by the free play of autonomous organizations within the state (the view of "true liberals" such as Montesquieu and Turgot). Some degree of division and discord—even of disorder—is a condition necessary to true freedom, both for the individual within the state and for the state among other states.

For Renan's abandonment of this classic "liberalism" in favor of a return to a quasi-feudal monarchism, in *La Réforme intellectuelle et morale,* the reasons are quite simple. He came to believe that the defeat of France by Prussia in 1870 was the fault of corrupt attitudes instilled in Frenchmen by their Revolution. France risked becoming a "second-rate America," and America meant for Renan an uncultured, if not barbaric, nation, devoted to nothing else but commerce. To emerge from anarchy domestically and to survive as a great nation internationally, France must reshape herself on the authoritarian and antidemocratic model of the very power that had defeated her: Prussia. *Revanche* thus becomes his battlecry in this work, not military revenge, but a more complex and subtle type (*revanche supérieure*), which consists of assimilating from a victorious enemy qualities that will enable her victim to emerge with renewed moral and intellectual superiority.

How did Doctor Renan hope to cure the ills of his patient, France? His title essay is divided into two parts: I. *Le Mal* and II. *Les remèdes.* The malady: weakness of moral fiber, owing in great part to the moral inefficacy of Catholic education; contempt for learning, and especially for the scientific knowledge without which, as Renan was shrewd enough to see, no modern nation could be militarily prepared (he also accuses Catholicism of this fault); materialism, equalitarianism, civic irresponsibility and lack of selfless devotion to the *patrie,* vices all to be blamed on the French Revolution. The remedies: restoration of a strongly authoritarian, though none the less constitutional, monarchy, enlightened enough to tell the people what is good for them, and supported by a hierarchy consisting of nobility (here for once Renan means nobility of birth), scientists and scholars, and army. The Church has a somewhat dubious place in this hierarchy, for the new French order, at least in its ruling élites, would be free-thinking and rationalist; yet the Catholic clergy would still remain useful as a means of keeping the populace in check. In brief, the "invisible aristocracy" of the *Essais de morale et de critique* has, in *La Réforme intellectuelle et morale,* been translated into an aristocracy that is only too visible and that, furthermore, is armed with the political means of reform, in an order of things that resembles both a parody of the *ancien régime* and a prototype of the fascist state.

The fallen France of *la débâcle* had, in Renan's eyes, reached an epic, an apocalyptic stage in her history which could be rendered only by poetic images borrowed from the Old Testament and from Greek mythology. Not since the Revolution of 1789, France's "epic poem" (*épopée*), had she known such a formidable crisis. The defeat of 1870 is a harvest reaped from almost a century of errors, but also an opportunity for France to "expiate" those errors, to "expiate the Revolution," to do penance with Prussia as her hair-shirt. The metaphors used in this book to describe the French nation in crisis are both startlingly down to earth and gloriously exalted. They range all the way from a "corpse rescued from the worms" to mythological heroes and gods, from a "putrefaction" (*pourriture*) to a providentially guided new Jerusalem, with Renan as her journalistic Isaiah— or, as he puts it more ironically, her "madman" crying "importunate truths" (*vérités importunes*) from the city's walls. France is a *Hercules in bivio* (at the crossroads), a Job "humiliated" only to be "exalted," a Prometheus punished by the Jupiter of a "harsh and proud Germanic virtue," but a Jupiter who may one day, in turn, "fall ignominiously."

IV *Fanatical Germanophile and Anti-Democrat?*

Two aspects of *La Réforme intellectuelle et morale* which have led to much misunderstanding call for explanatory comment: Renan's "Germanicism" and his attack on democracy.

The first of these has been the subject of much oversimplified and in fact nonsensical criticism in which Renan has been accused of being a naive Germanophile, a "traitor," a "collaborator" and the like. What are the facts, not merely as this one book reveals them but in the broad context of his whole work? As a young student, he had discovered a magnificent age of German philosophy and scholarship and had been completely justified in assimilating some of its major contributions to his own needs. Renan's achievement in adapting German thought to the French mind, in popularizing it, as Gabriel Séailles has pointed out, is comparable to that of Voltaire a century earlier, in relation to English thought.[4] How can this be a vice, when part of the greatness of French literature itself, from the sixteenth century onward, has been its power to seek out and absorb foreign in-

fluences, without destroying its originality? Long before 1870
Renan had been profoundly impressed by the respect for learning in Germany, by the religious character of its free-thought,
and in general by what he calls *le sérieux de cette race*. His program for educational reform, quite justifiably, looked in great
part to Germany as a model, especially for the strengthening of
scientific research.

Obviously it is the praise of Prussia in *La Réforme intellectuelle et morale* which has seemed to substantiate the charge that
he was a victim of the "German mirage." Yet even of this book
it is absolutely untrue to say that the image it presents of Germany is naively uncritical. Admittedly there is ambiguity, easily
misunderstandable, in the fact that by preaching emulation of
"Prussian virtues"—Protestant seriousness, hard work, and discipline—Renan gives the impression that he is blind to Prussian
vices and above all to the dangers posed to other states by
Prussian militaristic nationalism and expansionism. However, far
from ignoring these dangers, Renan has written on their subject
some of the most clairvoyant remarks to be found in the nineteenth century, vigorously denouncing what he calls the "racial
politics" and "political mysticism" of the young German nation.
He was hardly pleased to discover that German intellectuals in
uniform could pillage and burn along with the best of them.
He freely confesses that he had been under an illusion as to his
hope of friendship and cooperation between France and Germany.[5]

Yet, to Renan's lasting credit, he refused to give up this hope.
It was based on his belief that there are "two Germanies," the
gentler, more liberal and humanistic Germany of the "moral German" (*l'Allemand moral*) and the iron-handed, force-worship-
ping Germany of the "corrupt German" (*l'Allemand démoralisé*)
symbolized by "Prussia." The former, he also believed, would
eventually purge out the latter: *La Prusse passera, l'Allemagne
restera*. As naive as this hope may still have seemed after two
World Wars exacerbating Franco-German enmity, the post-
World War II history of Europe with its rapprochement of
France and Germany, its supra-national organizations and renewed dream of federation, has borne out the shrewdness of
Renan's vision. Were he alive today he could point with satisfac-
tion to prophetic passages of *La Réforme intellectuelle et morale*
calling for France and Germany to "hate each other as if one day
they would be allies," and predicting a "settling of accounts (*un*

règlement de comptes) ... for the good of the world between
these two great nations of central Europe." With equal shrewdness, Renan predicted that the Franco-German rapprochement
would be brought about by a political necessity: the need to
strengthen European unity as a kind of buffer (we would today
say a "third force") to offset the power of two new forces which
he perceived emerging on the world scene: the United States
and Russia.[6]

Renan objected to democracy on grounds similar to those
found in the works of other theorists of constitutional monarchy
in his century. A democratic state is subject to "the capricious
popular will," lacks direction and cultural distinction. It is incapable of providing the knowledge and discipline necessary to
wage modern warfare. Democracy's "original sin" is the sacrifices it must make to the "superficial crowd." Parliamentary
monarchy, on the other hand, expresses the "national will" (*la
volonté nationale*), and this, as distinct from the mere "popular
will" (*la volonté populaire*), is defined as "the result of the good
instincts of the people knowingly interpreted by reflective minds."
Yet for all this, it is impossible to class Renan as an unrelenting
opponent of the republican or democratic form of government.
He never denied absolutely that democracy might be a viable
and beneficent political system, even for Frenchmen. His reconciliation with the Third French Republic in the 1880's is to be
explained, not, as some of his critics have maintained, by cynical
opportunism, but in the light of two facts: (1) his political
thought, to begin with, was never a rigid set of theories, a closed,
doctrinaire system, but remained profoundly empirical in nature,
willing to judge political forms by what they actually achieve;
(2) as régimes went, the Third Republic compared favorably
with others he had known, allaying his fears of anarchy and the
destruction of culture. Though never more than lukewarm in his
positive estimate of democracy, he was willing to believe that
the saving grace outweighing all its defects (even in America)
might prove to be its conduciveness to the freedom of thought
which he prized so highly.[7]

Were Renan alive today, in the Fifth Republic of Charles de
Gaulle, would he consider Frenchmen finally to have achieved,
or still to be in search of, viable democracy? Once again, he
might reply by pointing to a prophetic sentence of *La Réforme
intellectuelle et morale:* "Monarchy is so natural to France that

any general who would give his country a striking victory would be capable of overthrowing republican institutions."

But let us return to the Third Republic.

V *Pessimism Rejected*

From 1879 to 1886, in his late fifties and early sixties, Renan delivered a number of speeches (*discours*) and lectures (*conférences*) to a variety of audiences and in a variety of settings: in the French Academy, to which he had been elected in 1878, and in the Sorbonne; to the Société des Etudes Juives and to the Cercle Saint-Simon; to scientists honoring his beloved Berthelot at a banquet in Paris and to Celticists honoring himself, and Brittany generally, at banquets in Tréguier and Quimper; to friends of the deceased Russian novelist, Turgenev, gathered in the Gare de Lyon, whence his remains were to be returned to his homeland; to graduating *lycéens* at Louis-le-Grand and to the Association des Etudiants. Gathered in book form as the *Discours et conférences*, only a few of these contributions have major importance, but all are, characteristically, readable in the highest degree. Beneath the great diversity of subject matter, a unifying thread is easily found: the author's continuing reflection upon the quality of contemporary French life.

Renan is still the lay preacher, the prophet. In his tribute to Michelet and Quinet, who had made brilliant use of the university to champion secularism, it becomes clear that Renan owes something to their tradition of *prédication laïque*, though his tone, above all in its light-heartedness, is extremely different from theirs. At one point he begs the Association des Etudiants to forgive him "this long lay sermon." As for prophecy, there are a number of references to the difficulty of being a "prophet" in the modern world; and the description of these collected speeches as "words thrown to the wind" (Préface, *paroles jetées au vent*) is vaguely reminiscent of Ezekiel's "prophesying unto the wind" (Chapter 37, Verse 9). But the prophet is no longer attacking *vulgarité* and *médiocrité*, no longer warning of some cataclysm; he is celebrating, with a gaiety that seems to rise from hidden depths of his character, France's rebirth from the dry bones of her ordeal of the 1870's. Gone, the invigorating pessimism of the *Essais de morale et de critique*, the *tristesse féconde* of *La Réforme intellectuelle et morale*, a sadness bordering at times—which is rare in Renan—on grimness. The *Discours et conférences* is an optimistic book, full of pleasure in the discovery

of the greatness of which Frenchmen were still capable, over-
flowing with the author's own joy in his life and labors. It is the
work, to apply to Renan his own phrase describing the Polish
poet Mickiewicz (who had been a colleague of Michelet and
Quinet at the Collège de France), of an "idealist stubborn despite every disappointment" (*idéaliste obstiné malgré toutes les
déceptions*).

To indicate some of the reasons why Renan took a more optimistic view of the French condition in the 1880's is also to sum
up the main themes of the book itself.

One reason, as I have already suggested, is certainly political.
In a humorous passage, but one which is essential to an understanding of his political thought, Renan sums himself up as a
légitimiste, that is, a person who needs "about ten years to ac-
custom myself to regarding any government as legitimate."
Revolutions, he adds, "have rendered this task difficult," for when
he is ready to accept a régime it is ready to fall. The fact, therefore, that the Republic seemed not at the point of collapsing
gave him great hope. "I, who am not a republican a priori, who
am a simple liberal (*un simple libéral*) quite willing to adjust
myself to a constitutional monarchy, would be more loyal to
the Republic than newly converted republicans" (*des républi-
cains de la veille*).

A second reason for the book's optimistic tone has to do with
the evolution of French philosophical thought in the 1880's. A
crisis, brought on in great part by the impact of science and positivism on traditional moral beliefs, had led many Frenchmen to
adopt a systematic pessimism, influenced by the German pes-
simistic philosophers, Schopenhauer and Hartmann. Pessimism
became a fashion, much like Existentialism after World War II.
Renan reacted with great vigor against this trend, especially as
it affected the young. To the students of Louis-le-Grand he said:
"Avoid the great evil of our time, that pessimism which prevents
your believing in unselfishness and virtue." A major goal of his
book is to provide ample reasons for refusing "to curse life." [8]

Renan himself, to touch upon a third reason for his brightened
outlook, had discovered evidence compelling him to revise his
view of his age as one dominated by "mediocrity and frivolity"
and to conclude that it was, instead, an age blessed with a large
measure of "unselfishness and virtue," even of the heroic kind.
The *Discours et conférences* celebrates several examples of such
greatness, including the scientists Pasteur, Berthelot, and Claude

Bernard, and the builder of the Suez Canal, Lesseps. The praise
of science—under which heading Renan includes philology and
history—is part of his reaffirmation in the 1880's (culminating
in the publication of *L'Avenir de la science*) of his belief that
the disinterested pursuit of truth, which "science" came to sym-
bolize for him, is the best means to happiness. For science provides "those scrupulous approximations, that successive refinement which brings us to viewpoints closer and closer to the
truth," a method which is "the very condition of the human
spirit." Its faith is a purely natural one, "not faith in particular
dogmas, but faith in humanity, in its brilliant destinies." Science
proves, through the examples of such unbelievers as Bernard,
Berthelot, and Littré, that the unselfish and virtuous life can be
led without belief in the supernatural and with the full exercise
of the critical faculty. To have left works, finally, that help "lead
the human spirit to the discovery of truth" is the only real immortality. Many eulogies of illustrious dead are pronounced in
this book, and the concern for death casts a shadow, though a
very gentle one, over its generally serene cheerfulness.

But Renan's renewed optimism was not dependent alone on
the number of great minds he perceived France to be still capable of producing. A fourth and final reason for it was his
awareness of profound popular sources of virtue and *honnêteté*
in the French nation itself—sources he is courageous enough to
admit that he may once have mistaken for weaknesses. He still
believes in an intellectual élite and writes with perception of
the increasing difficulty which *gens d'esprit* will experience in
attempting to influence democratic society for the good. "The
sum of reason which emerges from any given society to govern
it has always been feeble." But with age he had become a more
indulgent moralist, sensitive to the dangers of too much "moral
tension" and of an "excessive love for the good," convinced that
the smile (*le sourire*) has a moral value of its own. This relax-
ing of a position that had caused him earlier to insist somewhat
too much on *le sérieux* corresponds, in the 1880's, to the esthetic
"unbending" he had experienced thanks to his trip to Italy in
1849-1850.

To some extent his re-establishment of contact with his Breton
homeland accounted for this mellowing. Was he not a "son of
Pelagius," the heresiarch who had "done away with sin"? How
could a true Celt ever become a "pessimist" or a "nihilist"? Was
it not befitting a Celt to feel tolerance for each individual's "novel

of the infinite"? Even the levity, the *légèreté* he had once considered a defect of the *esprit français* (or more precisely of the
esprit gaulois which is one of its major components) he is now
willing to admit may be a virtue: *la vieille gaieté gauloise.* This
apparent reversal may have been the result of his epistolary
debate with Strauss in 1870, for it is in a letter to Strauss (whose
Germanic gravity he saw degenerating into "pedantry," "dogmatism," and "rigorism") that his reappraisal of the *esprit
français* first appears: "This frivolity for which we French are
reproached is at bottom serious and virtuous" (*Cette légèreté
qu'on nous reproche est au fond sérieuse et honnête*).[9]

But perhaps this "new Renan" is not so new, after all, and
is to be explained, above all, by something much simpler: the
natural ripening of a philosophy which, almost from the beginning, and despite a thick overlay of *sérieux,* had allied Renan
not with the more severe moralists but with "the wit, the gaiety,
the good intellectual health of a Lucian, a Montaigne, a Voltaire"
("Réponse au Discours de Pasteur"). Most men become insuf-
ferable puritans with age, to make up for their dissolute youth.
Renan, on the contrary, allows the *gaieté* which had always
been part of his nature to come abundantly to the surface, as
though to correct any excess of seriousness he may have been
guilty of as a young man. What had always been a matter of
temperament, he now elevates into a form of wisdom, of *sagesse.*

VI *Individual, Nation, and Humanity*

The part of *Discours et conférences* to which Renan attached
the greatest importance is his lecture entitled "What Is a Nation?" ("Qu'est-ce qu'une nation?"—Sorbonne, March 11, 1882).
At first glance it is not obvious how this essay fits into the book
as a whole. Yet it reveals itself to be as much the summation
and culminating point of the work as "La Poésie des races celtiques" had been for the *Essais de morale et de critique.* "I have
weighed each word of it," wrote Renan, "with the utmost care:
it is my profession of faith in all that concerns human affairs,
and, when modern civilization has foundered as a result of the
fatal misunderstanding of the words: 'nation,' 'nationality,' and
'race,' I hope these twenty pages will be remembered."

In this masterpiece of logical, orderly analysis—or "vivisec-
tion," as he wittily calls it—of the idea of a "nation," he throws
aside "metaphysical and theological abstractions" in order to get
at the reality of the "nation" empirically. The major error he

combats is the confusion of "nation" with "race." This is only one of several pseudo-definitions he rejects. A nation does not rest, as German theorists of expansionism would have it in their attempt to justify the annexing of territories "racially" related to theirs, upon an "anthropological" or "zoological" basis (a reference to the dispute over Alsace). Nor do a common language or religion, common commercial interests, military necessity, or natural geographical frontiers, provide us with the essential "national principle." There are too many thriving exceptions to each of these alleged criteria for any one of them to be decisive.

A nation is finally defined as a "spiritual principle." It is based on the possession, as a great "spiritual family," of a common legacy of memories concerning the past, and on a continuing will to remain together in present and future. It is thus a form of "moral consciousness." In a brilliant metaphor, Renan defines the nation as "a daily plebiscite" (*un plébiscite de tous les jours*), and adds that in this respect it resembles the existence of the individual person, which is also "a perpetual affirmation of life." But here, worthy to be quoted in full, is the key passage:

> Man cannot improvise his being (*L'homme ne s'improvise pas*). The nation, like the individual, is the result of a long past made up of efforts, of sacrifices, of devoted attachments. The cult of one's ancestors is the most legitimate of all cults; our ancestors have made us what we are. A heroic past, great men, glory (I mean the true kind), this is the social capital on which one founds the idea of a nation. To have common glories in the past, and a common will in the present; to have done great things together and to wish to do more, these are the conditions essential for being a people.

Just as Renan believed in science but not in the cult of science, so he believed in the nation but not in nationalism.[10] True patriotism, as he himself exemplified it, is the courage to declare one's nation mistaken when one believes that to be the truth. Pseudo-patriotism is to the nation what vanity is to the individual. The world risks being plunged into "wars of extermination" by too ardent nationalists or those he contemptuously calls "transcendental politicians." Although he considers "the principle of nationhood just and legitimate," he also suggests that nations are not eternal and that one day a larger family of loyalties might replace them. The highest "ideal reality" in which Renan believed was not the nation but humanity. "Human culture," he reminds us, antedates and is greater than national cultures. In

one of his noblest sentences, worth pondering in our own age
when the revival of nationalism coincides with the loss of faith
in man's rationality and power for good, he cautions thus: "Let
us not abandon this fundamental principle, namely, that man is
a reasonable and moral being, before being enclosed (*parqué*)
in such and such a language, and before being a member of
such and such a race, or an adherent of such and such a culture."

CHAPTER 7

Play of Ideas

"S TORE up for your lives," Renan advised a group of French students in 1886, "an ample provision of good humor. Except for cases of national disaster, make allowance for the smile and for the hypothesis that this world may not be a very serious matter (*l'hypothèse où ce monde ne serait pas quelque chose de bien sérieux*). Surely in any case the world is delightful as it is." Airy mockery of solemn issues, light-hearted play with themes which others more traditionally have treated in noble or tragic or anguished style—these qualities become more and more apparent in the works Renan wrote beginning roughly in 1870; they find their highest expression in the *Dialogues philosophiques* (1876), the *Drames philosophiques* (1878-1886), and in portions of *Souvenirs d'enfance et de jeunesse* (1883). The "benevolent universal irony" (*bienveillante ironie universelle*) so characteristic of the later Renan sometimes depends for its effect on a single phrase, as in the example cited: *hors les cas de désastre national;* the very choice of the plural noun is ironic, as though France could go on surviving any number of disasters without help from its intellectuals; and how can one take this supposed exception seriously if the world itself may be no more than a joke? Sometimes the irony is more delicate, for, unlike that which scintillates in the short, dry sentences of Voltaire or Stendhal, it may turn up in the midst of an otherwise "straight" passage of lyrical or oratorical prose, causing its whole message to deflect mischievously.

I *Renanisme*

This vein of writing, often called *renanisme,* has provoked divergent reactions from critics: some see it as the culmination of his wisdom and literary art; others condemn it as a form of decadence, symptomatic of the late nineteenth century's decline into that irresponsible, sensuous, and superficial playing with ideas which they contemptuously call "dilettantism." These

severe judges (Massis, Parigot, Chaix-Ruy, and others) accuse
Renan of subverting the moral purpose of the young, indeed of
a much worse crime, betraying the youthful moral idealist strug-
gling to survive in himself.

In an earlier book, I attempted to relate *renanisme* to Renan's
"fear of being duped," interpreting it with some sympathy, but
not very positively, as an elaborate device, like some multi-
layered mask or heavily encoded message, designed to conceal
beneath apparent frivolity an idealism still strong, still persistent,
despite many disappointments.[1] Though this interpretation preserves, I believe, an element of truth, a simpler explanation,
more in harmony with what I have come to discover as the
fundamental unity and consistency of Renan's whole work, is
now worth proposing. It is this: the ironic play of ideas is an
aspect of Renan's thought which is deeply rooted in his whole
temperament and outlook. Far from being a betrayal of his earlier work, a puzzling volte-face, a sign of decadence, it is the
fulfillment of a tendency present from the beginning. It is the
long-delayed expression *in literary form* of an activity of mind
often described or alluded to, but seldom practiced, before the
1870's.

II   Seeds of Ideological Play

The view of life as an amusing ideological spectacle was already contained, in germ, in the cult of "humanity" with which
Renan, in the 1840's, replaced the cult of the absolute God of
Catholic theism. For, by affirming the need to grasp humanity's
experience in all its fullness (*Le sublime serait d'embrasser le
tout à tous ses points de vue*), the author of the *Cahiers de
jeunesse* and *L'Avenir de la science* was opening the way to the
juxtaposition and confrontation in his work of multiple and contradictory points of view. It is most revealing to compare a
passage of his *Principes de conduite* (December 1843; he still
clung, though uneasily, to his faith), deploring as a weakness his
habit of defending ideas in which he does not believe ("This
is making sport of the truth," *c'est se jouer avec la vérité*), with
a number of passages of very different tone in *L'Avenir de la
science*. Among the latter may be cited: (1) the description of
"criticism" as "discoursing on all the surfaces of things, wander-
ing as a multiple observer in a corner of universal being" (*se
promener en observateur multiple dans un coin de l'universel*);
(2) the characterization (from Pythagoras by way of Cicero) of

the philosopher as spectator, rather than participant, in the game of life; (3) the defense of "philosophical laughter" (*le rire philosophique*, to be distinguished carefully from *plaisanterie*, which is unphilosophical because tending to ridicule), as an attitude consistent with the highest form of criticism.

However, there is little "laughter" in *L'Avenir de la science*, with its youthful impatience to reshape society by the rule of reason. "One must always do one's best and do it as soon as possible," is a sentence from that work which might serve as its admirable motto. The view of life as the object of reform calling for the scholar's active commitment seems contradicted by the view of life as a theater of ideas to be enjoyed with detached amusement.

A similar contradiction, a similar hesitancy to accept fully, as a strength, the critical power of acknowledging multiple points of view, characterize *Patrice*, an unfinished confessional "novel" in epistolary form, dating from 1849. The subject of this *fragment romanesque* is the conflict between Patrice, representing Renan's new-found "criticism," and the young woman he loves, Cécile, who continues to profess the uncritical religious faith that also lies buried in the conscience of Patrice himself. In content, though hardly in form, this work anticipates strikingly some essential elements of the "play of ideas." Patrice defines criticism as the "maintaining of contradictory elements in opposition, so as not to let a single component of humanity stifle any other." He frankly admits that his own hospitality to contradictory ideas would have prevented his being a successful martyr: had he been Saint Catherine he would have told the philosophers persecuting him, "Let us agree; yes, in a sense, you are right: I am quite willing to sacrifice to Jupiter." The good-humored irony of this passage even foreshadows the very tone of *renanisme*. But the most striking anticipation which this early work affords of the "vintage" Renan occurs in a footnote which Renan added to explain Patrice's paradoxical remark that only a "petty mind" would wish to "do away with evil": "In reading this passage one must remember that Patrice does not always express definitively fixed opinions, but insights (*aperçus*) of whose imperfection he was well aware, but which he judged capable by their very error of opening up new views and provoking thought (*faire réfléchir*)." We are uncannily close here, in this footnote of 1849, to the *Dialogues philosophiques* of 1876, with its use of "exaggerations" in order to "stimulate reflection" (*exciter à réfléchir*).

During what might be called Renan's "middle period," in the
1850's and 1860's, the favorable response of a wide reading public
to his unique mixture of skepticism and idealism strengthened
his belief that the critical spirit, the ironic smile, were consistent
with high moral purpose and true religious feeling. To demon-
strate this belief is one of the major purposes of the *Etudes
d'histoire religieuse* and *Essais de morale et de critique*. The
latter work is rich in foreshadowings of the play of ideas, especially in its frequent references to the philosopher's right to view
the world as "spectacle," without concern for the consequences
of his speculations. The emphasis on the value of disinterested
contemplation in this book is not due wholly to Renan's love of
contemplation; it is also to be explained as resignation to the
de facto powerlessness of the "man of thought" in the modern
bureaucratic state (specifically, in 1859, the quasi-dictatorship
of Napoleon III). The association of the play of ideas with political pessimism, so characteristic of both *Dialogues* and *Drames
philosophiques*, is already distinctly evident here. "Contemplation" becomes a means of asserting, in the autonomous realm of
ideas, the freedom he knew to be more and more conditioned
in the realm of politics. Perhaps it is even the "thinker's" way of
avenging the frustrated "man of action."

If a successful political career means limiting one's philosophical freedom, as the example of Cousin seemed to prove, then
Renan has no choice but to reaffirm this freedom. He does so
("M. Cousin," *Essais de morale et de critique*) with a certain
boldness, placing the philosopher, as Nietzsche will do, "beyond
good and evil": "The philosopher's nature is not to think of consequences, or, more precisely, it is to raise speculation to that
height from which any evil consequence is banished, and does
not even present itself to thought. Once he has reached this
degree of maturity and goodness, which study gives him, the
thinker is so to speak reduced to the impossibility of doing evil."
Even supposing the worst about the world—that it is "the night-
mare of a sick God or an accidental appearance on the surface
of nothingness"—it is still fully justified as an object of the philosopher's *curiosité*, still "the strangest and most delightful of
spectacles." Again, it is as though Renan were already carrying
the *dialogues* and the *drames* in his head.

La pensée pour la pensée, "thought for thought's sake," one
might call this argument, for it occupies a place in Renan's
scheme of things analogous to that of "art for art's sake" in the

poet Gautier's. But Renan goes even further, still within the framework of the *Essais de morale et de critique*. He not only claims that the pleasure of playing with ideas is a valid end in itself; he also claims that this approach provides a better chance of discovering the truth than an absolutist spirit, determined too intently on reaching "conclusions." The harm done to thinking by the need to "conclude" had already occupied his attention a few years earlier, in the Preface to *Averroès et l'averroïsme:* "Critical judgment excludes dogmatic judgment. Who knows if true finesse of mind does not consist in refraining from reaching a conclusion?" (*Qui sait si la finesse d'esprit ne consiste pas à s'abstenir de conclure?*).

In the *Essais* it is Lamennais, even more than Cousin, who furnishes the antithesis of the play of ideas. His habit of thinking in a straight line (*pensée en ligne droite*), his lack of *raillerie* (jesting, bantering), not only deprived him of the pleasure of *libres promenades dans le monde de l'esprit,* but also kept him from capturing the very truth he was hunting down. Like all "men of action" Lamennais sought too tensely to save the world, not realizing that only by being willing to "do without the world" can one hope to reform it. *La vérité,* after all, is a woman, "one of those capricious women whom one loses, so they say [!], for loving them too much." A certain "air of indifference," even a "degree of coldness," succeed better than grave adoration, in philosophy as in love. To change the metaphor, Lamennais "rushed upon the truth with the heavy impetuosity of a wild boar: fugitive and light-footed truth turned aside, and, for lack of suppleness, he kept missing her." [2]

III *To Imagine Something New*

Why, if all the essential components of the play of ideas were present in earlier works (as I believe they were), did the literary forms most suitable to its expression take so long in gestating? The closest that Renan himself came to answering this question was to say that he had earned the right to levity, in the last few decades of his life, as a reward for the austere hard work of his youth. Although this does not suffice to explain the genesis of the *Dialogues* and *Drames philosophiques* (the man who, almost until his death, labored to complete *Histoire du peuple d'Israël,* could hardly have lost all continuity with his *sérieuse jeunesse*), it is nevertheless true that the aging Renan welcomed moments of relaxation and diversion from the intense purposefulness of

his work, and that these moments also provided him with what
he had already referred to, in *Essais de morale et de critique,* as
"the leisure to think at one's ease." Such leisure, to which we owe
the inspiration of at least three works of ideological play, was
not always a matter of his own choice; it was imposed upon him
by the contingencies of his existence. The *Dialogues philosophiques* were written in 1871 at Versailles, separated from his
books, in temporary exile from a Paris under siege. The first and
second of the four philosophical dramas, *Caliban* and *L'Eau de
Jouvence,* were composed at the watering station of Ischia, an
island in the Bay of Naples, where Renan periodically sought
relief from the pains of rheumatism.

However, despite the context of political catastrophe or physical suffering in which they were conceived, the *dialogues* and
drames testify to an extraordinary renewal of spiritual vitality
on the part of a Renan of whom Jean Pommier has said that his
"brain remained young in a prematurely aged body." [3] They go
further than any of his other works in evoking the grimmest possibilities for mankind, while at the same time reaffirming un-
mistakably his hope in mankind. Thus, the significance, in the
Preface to the *Dialogues,* of the reference to the Marquis de
Condorcet, at the height of the Terror, awaiting death in his
prison cell while writing his *Sketch of the Progress of the Human
Spirit.* Somber though individual scenes or themes of the *drames*
may be, the light that illuminates them is that of an Ischia morn-
ing "when the vines were covered with dew and the sea was like
whitish watered silk"; the philosophy that redeems even their
most sardonic insights into the human condition is that of the
"crickets and larks, who have never doubted that sunlight is
sweet, life an excellent gift, and the land of the living a most
agreeable place to sojourn."

But these works also testify—more to the point of our inquiry
into their timing in Renan's literary calendar—to an equally extraordinary literary renewal on his part. Having already shown
his mastery of the historical form and of the essay, he perceived
that the key to his rejuvenation, in his mid-fifties, lay in a freer
play of the fancy. Buoyed up by the examples of those eternally
young Romantics, Hugo and George Sand, who proved that
"genius knows no old age," as well as by the efforts of those
closer to him in age—Taine, Flaubert, Claude Bernard, Marcellin
Berthelot—to surpass themselves, he wrote: "I feel within me a
youthfulness and ardor; I wish to imagine something new: (*Je*

sens en moi quelque chose de jeune et d'ardent; je veux imaginer quelque chose de nouveau)." To this intensified use of the imagination lying at the heart of his "second youth" we owe the masterpieces of his final period: *Souvenirs d'enfance et de jeunesse*, with its blending of a variety of literary forms to serve an autobiographical purpose; *Dialogues* and *Drames philosophiques* to the analysis of which I now turn.

IV *Lobes of a Brain Conversing*

Besides the play of ideas suggested by their very titles, these two works have in common their "philosophical" matter, a term broad enough to include for Renan both traditional problems of philosophy and those of a political nature. "I used these moments of forced leisure," he explains, "to effect a return upon myself (*faire un retour sur moi-même*) and to draw up a kind of summary (*une sorte d'état sommaire*) of my philosophical beliefs." This "summary" has, in the dialogues, something of the logical structure which persists beneath the apparent vagaries of most philosophical dialogues; in the dramas (the change actually begins in the third dialogue, *Rêves*) the thought unfolds in a much less clear and logical fashion, and borders at times on a novel (for Renan) and daring kind of controlled incoherence. But, whatever their differences of detail, both works, as distinct from the more straightforward expression of his ideas in essays and histories, enable us to view in a different lighting—precisely that of the play of ideas—the philosophical questions that never ceased to preoccupy Renan: the nature of God; the origins and destiny of man; the purpose or purposelessness of history; the concern for survival after death; the future of science and religion in a democratic society—a concern which involves both the fate of the cultivated man of reason, the "natural aristocrat," and the fate of the masses no longer guided by traditional religious beliefs, by *les vieilles croyances*.

Had certain critics of Renan read the Preface of the *Dialogues philosophiques* more carefully they would have avoided the error of attributing to Renan, as his definitive beliefs, all the opinions expressed by whatever participants. For he painstakingly explains that he chose the dialogue form precisely because "it has nothing dogmatic about it and allows one to present in succession the diverse aspects of a problem, without being obliged to conclude." His sole purpose has been "to stimulate reflection (*exciter à réfléchir*), sometimes even to arouse the reader's philosophical sense by certain exaggerations." No one of the characters (cf. the device common in the traditional dialogue) is a pseudonym for the author or for any of his contemporaries, although he does grant that they *all* represent different sides of his thought in its varying degrees of "certitude, probability, and dream." "Peaceful dialogues," Renan describes this work, in a phrase that has become famous, "in which the different lobes of my brain have a habit of indulging, when I let them go astray with perfect freedom" (*ce sont les pacifiques dialogues auxquels ont coutume de se livrer les différents lobes de mon cerveau, quand je les laisse divaguer en toute liberté*).

Exagérations, rêveries, divaguer (which means not only "going astray" but also "being incoherent")—it is obvious from his choice of words that Renan would guard the reader against taking everything he says with equal seriousness, as the voice of reason. Euthyphron remarks to Philalèthe: "We make allowance in your thought for a certain paradoxical form, whose purpose is to render the thought more palpable, and for an irony which you justly hold to be very philosophical. . . . You would even be capable of affecting vice, so as not to appear pharisaical in a hypocritical age like ours where there is an advantage in being right-thinking (*bien pensant*)." The main problem in interpreting the *Dialogues*—something apart from merely enjoying them as a display of intellectual fireworks—thus becomes one of reconciling their author's playfulness with his avowed purpose of "drawing up a summary of his philosophical beliefs"; it is the problem of deciding which ideas, and with what degree of conviction, belong to the ego which controls the master switch of the conversing *lobes du cerveau.*

Renan goes a long way toward helping us resolve this enigma by introducing two features which also, incidentally, tend to restrict the freedom which he accords to the play of ideas. He has divided the work into three parts, entitled respectively *Certitudes, Probabilités,* and *Rêves.* He has also given to each of his five interlocutors a symbolic name and has chosen three of them, whose names signify in part "God" or "truth," to carry the burden of each dialogue. Philalèthe, "lover of truth," expounds "certitudes"; Théophraste, "teller, informer of, guide to, God," suggests "probabilities"; Théoctiste, "founder, establisher of God," projects in the form of "dreams" the shape of things to come. On the other hand, Euthyphron, the practical man with "plain, honest, straightforward understanding," and Eudoxe, representing repu-

table "opinions" (especially philosophical) as opposed to "knowledge," ask questions, raise doubts and objections, and serve
as sounding boards for the paradoxes of the three natural
theologians.

Beliefs accepted by Philalèthe as certainties are only two in
number—exactly two more, however, than Renan has been allowed by superficial critics who perpetuate the myth that he
believed in nothing. He affirms, first, the nonexistence of any
being superior to man and capable of intervening in nature or
history. "God" is on no one's side, or rather, "the alleged God
of armies is always on the side of the nation with the best artillery
and the best generals." (Twentieth-century readers please substi-
tute, "the best nuclear force.") Yet with every bit as much conviction as Philalèthe-Renan denies supernatural "government"
he also affirms (his second certitude) that "the world has a purpose and labors at a mysterious work" (*le monde a un but et
travaille à une œuvre mystérieuse*). This universal striving toward
higher forms of life, toward greater "consciousness" (*conscience*),
Philalèthe compares to the movement of plants toward water
and light, the emergence of the embryo from its matrix, or the
metamorphoses of the insect. He draws two corollaries from this
second certitude: nature uses us, whether we will or no, toward
this higher goal; the wisest attitude is not that of revolt, but that
of conformity, in the Stoic sense, to nature's purpose. To persist
in virtue, in unselfish love, in the taste for goodness and truth,
is to become the "willing dupes" of the universal *nisus* (effort),
the universal *fieri* (becoming), out of which God is emerging.
"Man," writes Renan, in the most famous of a rich profusion of
images intended to show the benevolent "Machiavellianism" of
nature, "is like the operator at the Gobelin tapestry works, weaving the reverse side of a tapestry whose design he does not see."

It is when Renan, with Théophraste, moves from these certainties about nature to the question of how human history reveals
(if at all) progress toward *conscience*, that he enters the realm
of probabilities. In a curious mixture of metaphors from applied
mathematics, business, and biology, Théophraste envisions history as a geometrical sum (*une résultante*), an amassing of capi-
tal funds (*une capitalisation*), a slow accumulation of spiritual
goods, marked by enormous waste (*déperditions*) but also by
endless surpluses (*surcroîts*), as in "adolescent nutrition." When
Euthyphron raises the vexing possibility that mankind is decaying
rather than progressing (democracy may reduce our ardor for

virtue and truth just as the diminishing coal supply may cause
the planet to grow cold), Théophraste replies that the fulfillment
of reason may lie not by way of democracy but by way of a hier-
archized society controlled by an élite and based on recognition
of the incurable inequality of individuals and of races. His hypothesis that the triumph of reason may best be achieved by
a scientific élite empowered with absolute political and military
control, his references to thinking machines, eugenic breeding,
artificial determination of sex, and the perfecting of scientific
weaponry, his recognition that art, poetry, beauty, and virtue
may simply become extinct—all this reads like a deliberate
parody by Renan of his own *Future of Science.*

This caricatural element ("caricature" is from the Italian
caricare, "to exaggerate, to load") assumes ever weirder shapes
in *Rêves.* We are forewarned about Théoctiste, the organizer of
dreams, at the end of *Probabilités.* "Théoctiste exaggerates his
views and makes the mistake of trying to trace precise images
of what can only be vaguely perceived; but rays of light sometimes break through his somber cloud. . . ." *Rêves* may well be
the most original and powerful of the three dialogues. As Jean
Onimus has pointed out, the device of the dream allowed Renan
to put aside the nuances and qualifications, the "fine approximations" of his rational thought, and to indulge in bold fantasies
voicing the irrational, if not the subconscious, side of his being.
Onimus highlights an even more remarkable aspect of the third
dialogue: these nineteenth-century "nightmares" (*mauvais rêves,
cauchemars,* as Renan himself calls them) of an idealism that
allows reason to be pushed to irrational lengths, have since been
translated into some of the twentieth century's most horrifying
realities.[4] The "dreamer" Théoctiste is also a prophet, with un-
canny relevance to our own time. The basic problem with which
he copes turns out to be one of the most profound of our century:
the struggle between democratic and totalitarian forms to shape
the future and achieve the well-being of humanity.

Whereas Théophraste had tended to dwell upon the "inequality of races," Théoctiste's function is to evaluate political forms
—democracy, oligarchy, monarchy—in the light of the "future of
consciousness." He is one of Renan's most zealous eliminators
of democracy.[5] "It is not very likely," he informs us, "that God
will come about through democracy." The ideal of American
society, in particular, "is perhaps [the adverb mitigates his zeal
somewhat] further removed than any other from the ideal of a

society governed by knowledge (*science*)." The "theological error" of democracy is to fail to reckon with the inherent inequality of men and to believe that the masses will ever be enlightened enough to rule with any degree of directness. "Pure reason" will become incarnate not (to update his vocabulary a bit) in the "brotherhood" of all men but in the super-humanity of a few. Théoctiste's visions become more monstrous as he warms to his subject. He foresees the concentration of power in the hands of an oligarchy who, thanks to their application of science to armaments, will assume "universal dominion" over the rest of men, acquiring a force great enough "to destroy the planet." The ancient aristocratic and ecclesiastical dream of absolute spiritual power will at last become a reality; a "truly infallible papacy" of "positivist tyrants" (*tyrans positivistes*), men become like gods (*dévas*, Sanskrit for "deities"), will rule the world in the name of reason.

Despite the vague allusion to Germany as foreshadowing this totalitarian order, the description seems best to fit neither Nazism nor Fascism but Communism. Hegel was, after all, a source common to Renan and Marx; and the influence of Hegel is felt in the *Dialogues* to the point where Renan seems at times to be parodying both himself and Hegel. An oligarchy which rules for the purpose of achieving a "classless society" is not far different from Théoctiste's oligarchy which rules in the name of "incarnate reason." Yet the most striking originality of Renan's prophecies lies not so much in his foreshadowing of those totalitarian forms which have become traditional as in his prediction that the armaments race would profoundly alter the nature of *all political forms* in the direction of oligarchical dictatorship and away from democracy. Here the key sentence is this: "The perfecting of arms leads to the opposite of democracy; it tends to strengthen not the masses (*la foule*), but the government in power, since scientific arms serve governments, not peoples."

The final, most curious dream of this "founder of God" is his vision of a kind of pantheistic absolute monarchy, in which one superman among supermen will emerge as the most perfect, a rationalist "messiah," a quintessence of intellect, who in his single miraculously developed brain will concentrate all that humanity is capable of feeling. Even more astonishingly, he will clothe himself with the very universe, becoming "an infinite polyp, to which all the beings that have ever existed will be soldered by their base, living simultaneously their own lives and the life of

the whole." Renan's "idealist philosopher," who began quietly in
the first dialogue with a quotation from the Christian rationalist,
Malebranche, has here attained the proportions of a Rabelaisian
giant, of Hugo's *Satyre*, almost of Lautréamont's pre-surrealistic
Maldoror. Yet with sure esthetic sense Renan knows well enough
not to conclude the dialogues on this fantastic note. In his final
remarks, Théoctiste, leaving behind both "somber images" of the
future and mystico-erotic daydreams, comes back to earth with
a self-portrait—which is also a portrait of Renan—describing
how he has lived the life of humanity in himself and achieved
some kind of meaningful immortality. The calm climax of this
epilogue is reached with a reaffirmation of the idea of God as
the "immobile center," the fixed rational core, of the universe.
Malebranche returns at the end, but to be crossed with Hegel:
"God will be and God is. As reality, he will be; as ideal, he is.
God is both being and becoming (*Deus est simul in esse et in
fieri*)."

V   *A Theater of Ideas*

The *Drames philosophiques* grew out of the *Dialogues* as their
sequel and necessary completion. Restating his belief, in his
Preface to the *Collected Dramas* (1888), that the dialogue form
is best suited to the expression of ideas whose truth can be
neither affirmed nor denied with certainty, Renan nevertheless
progresses beyond dialogue to a sharper means of rendering the
"doubts and half-lights, the insolences followed by retreats (*les
audaces suivies de reculs*), the comings and goings" of his philosophical thought. For if the essence of dialogue is to "set in
motion diverse opinions" (*mettre en jeu des opinions diverses*),
the essence of drama is to "set in opposition different types"
(*opposer des types différents*). Plato's dialogues already possessed much of the quality of philosophical drama, with living,
well-rounded characters. Renan's quintet of philosophers, on the
other hand, are little more than symbolic names, mere voices for
ideas that exist, despite their application to the modern world,
as abstractions. Abandoning dialogue for drama is his way of
reminding us that ideas, historically, are bound up with flesh
and blood human beings, and that "ideological" conflicts are
seldom purely ideological. "Whatever implies a nuance of faith,
of deliberate adherence, of choice, of antipathy, of sympathy, of
hatred or love, is best cast in a form of expression where each

opinion is incarnated in a person and has the bearing of a living being."

The contrast could hardly be more striking between the ghostly philosophers who speak for Renan's "brain lobes" in a remote corner of a Versailles park (a suitable "no-place," and, were it not for the pregnant allusion to the year 1871, a "no-time"), and the scores of characters, men and women, great and small, cultured and illiterate, named and nameless, who crowd the scenes of his philosophical dramas. In relating how he was compelled to follow up the first of his dramas with its sequel, he refers, not to the somewhat impersonal *lobes de son cerveau,* but, like a true dramatist obsessed by his characters, to "those beloved images [Caliban, Prospero, Ariel]" which "began to converse among themselves in my mind." The dramas represent a distinct advance in the liberation of Renan's imaginative powers. They also reveal his desire to create a more complete image of the world than he had given us to date. Love between the sexes is finally recognized: "I have wished my work to be the mirror of the universe (*l'image de l'univers*); I have been obliged to provide a place for love." Women play no role in the almost sexless dialogues: "This superior world of which we dream for the coming of pure reason would have no women in it" (Théoctiste). In the dramas, women emerge with ever-increasing importance.

Caliban (1878), conceived as a sequel to Shakespeare's *Tempest,* relates how the plebeian creature and slave of the alchemist, Prospero, overthrows the latter's aristocratic dictatorship-in-the-name-of-reason in order to set up a democracy, and how, in a curious progression, he "glimpses good for the first time," and, from the anti-clerical and enemy of culture he had been in the beginning, becomes—ironically—a "moderate" and a protector of both science and the church. In this play, Renan, using the symbolic figures provided by Shakespeare, pursues his speculation on the problem that had absorbed him in the *Dialogues* and other works: the future of democracy. More precisely, what will be its relation to older aristocratic values of church and learning? Can "civilization"—an aristocratic creation—survive democracy? Can "reason" shape human affairs only by being imposed from above by an enlightened dictator? Or can the people ever become rational enough to exercise wise self-rule? None of these questions is fully answered; the play's ending is an "open" one: "Caliban perhaps has a future" (*Caliban a peut-être de l'avenir*), "one must wait and see" (*il faut attendre*).

L'Eau de Jouvence (1881), or *Fountain of Youth*, the sequel
to *Caliban*, has a more complex plot, with two principal and not
very well-fused motifs. The political problem raised in *Caliban*
is apparently resolved when Prospero, sensing his death approach
and still affirming the legitimacy of his rule, nevertheless urges
his servant Ariel, or pure spirit, to "cease scorning Caliban."
Aristocracy and democracy are reconciled when Prospero recognizes the two "consciousnesses" at work in humanity: the *conscience claire* of the élite and the *conscience obscure* of the
people. Even Caliban's "gruntings" (*grognements*) represent "a
principle of forward movement in humanity." (The Foreword
or *Au lecteur* had prepared us for this dénouement: "Let us keep
Caliban; let us try to find a means to give Prospero an honorable
burial and to attach Ariel to life. . . .") The second motif, already suggested in the title, is the pursuit of eternal youth, both
on the part of Pope Clement, a delightful rascal anxious to preserve his virile ardor for his mistress (and seeking to exploit
Prospero's alchemy to this end), and on the part of Prospero,
intent, with more dignity, on finding what *l'eau de Jouvence*
symbolizes: "an ideal which prevents one from aging." Quite
probably Renan means to contrast in these two figures the old
aristocracy of a decaying church and the new aristocracy of that
modern alchemist we call the scientist. His own concern for survival after death, and for a "beautiful death," increasingly obvious
in this play, prepares the way for further "play" with this idea
in *L'Abbesse de Jouarre*.

The dominant motif of *Le Prêtre de Némi* (1885), probably
the best constructed and most truly dramatic of the four plays
(it borders indeed at times on melodrama), Renan owed to the
ancient Greek geographer, Strabo: the legend of the priest-king
who is obliged to kill his predecessor in order to consecrate his
own rule, the sacred murder being repeated from generation to
generation.[6] With brilliant irony, Renan imagines a reasonable
and idealistic priest, Antistius, who comes to power without
committing this ritual slaying; his ambition to rule in the name
of reason throws all into disorder; he is finally slain by a more
orthodox successor, and "order" returns (*tout rentre dans l'ordre*).
A subordinate but important motif involves the war between
Némi and Alba-Longa: the criminal heresy of Antistius is all the
more heinous, in the eyes of the "demagogues," since he refuses
to pursue this war with the prescribed fanaticism, being governed
not by national patriotism but by *le patriotisme de l'humanité*.

The plight of poor Antistius, as much ahead of his times in the nineteenth century as he had been in the age of Romulus and Remus, or as he would be in our own, serves Renan as the vehicle for some of the most devastating attacks on super-patriotism and military "heroism" in all of literature.

The last of the dramas, *L'Abbesse de Jouarre* (1886), seems at first glance to suggest a complete break with the type of subject, the tone, indeed the whole inspiration, of the earlier plays. The number of characters is reduced severely, almost to the level of a French classical tragedy, becoming essentially a *drame à deux*. Adapted from the true history of a worldly eighteenth-century abbess's last hours as a prisoner condemned to death by the Terror, the play concerns an aristocratic nun's confrontation with death, her love for a fellow aristocrat condemned to die with her, her renouncing the vow of chastity in the shadow of death, and her discovery of the sacred character of motherhood. Yet markedly different though the play is from the others in its greater respect for scenic conventions and for a certain "realism," in its sentimentality, and in the greater degree of mystery, if not of obscurity, surrounding the author's intentions, it may not be so detached as it first appears from the trio preceding it.

The *Drames philosophiques* are in fact linked together by several recurrent themes: priesthood (symbolizing spiritual or intellectual vocation) in relation to populace; revolt; sexuality; death. Prospero is a priest of science, Antistius a priest of reason, Julie de Saint-Florent, the Abbess of Jouarre, a freethinker among abbesses, who becomes a priestess of natural instinct. These idealists exemplify their creator's conviction that "moral nobility does not depend on metaphysical beliefs." They are all *purs*. Antistius, indeed, is too pure, too absolute an idealist, in his failure to allow for the function of tradition in any viable society. "Here," cautions Renan, "I am pleading a bit against myself" (*Ici, je plaide un peu contre moi-même*). Strangely enough, the Renan of empirical adjustment to established régimes also seems to be "pleading against himself" in his obsession with the theme of revolt: Caliban's revolt against exploitation by aristocracy; Antistius's revolt against a cruel dogma; and most extreme of all, Julie's defiance of what must have still been, for nineteenth-century readers, a very strong taboo, namely, social conventions governing sexual propriety.

For the increasing attention he granted to the sexual theme—
Pope Clement and Brunissende; Antistius and the sibyll Carmenta; above all, *L'Abbesse de Jouarre,* the whole action of
which is postulated on the ennobling of sexual intercourse—
Renan has been accused of becoming a libidinous old man betraying a long-suppressed and secret vulgarity. The truth may
be much less sensational: he may simply be according, in his
fuller "image of the universe," a more deserved place to the
natural instinct of sex, not as pure instinct, but as a "divine"
instrument for achieving spiritual ends. The meaning of this
theme for the man, Renan, as distinct from the playwright who
can imagine what he will, remains somewhat obscure.

The personal significance for him of the theme of death, on
the other hand—from Prospero's achievement of a happy death
to round out a "life arranged according to the rules of harmonious proportion (*eurythmie*)" to the drama of Julie—is quite
clear. "The hour of death is essentially philosophical. . . . The
necessary condition of the dialogue is the sincerity of its characters. And the hour of death is the most sincere of all." [7] By
imagining joyous sexual union in the shadow of the scaffold, by
allowing his Prospero to die "gradually extinguished," calling for
tunes from Amalfi and the Gulf of Naples and with a smile of
infinite pleasure, Renan upsets the Christian myth of life's culminating in a grand act of repentance, to return to the Stoic ideal
of arranging to die "when one wished" and "intact, sound of
mind and body, without prior debilitation." He is firmly ruling
out, as he will again in the final pages of *Souvenirs d'enfance
et de jeunesse,* the possibility of his own deathbed conversion.

Another way of discovering the unity underlying the *Drames
philosophiques,* at least the first three, for all their individual
profusion of ideas, is to consider them as so many efforts to
confront, lucidly and without self-deception or hypocrisy, some
extreme hypotheses concerning mankind's corruption and stupidity; and yet, having confronted these evils, to reaffirm one's
faith in the survival of reason and virtue. "The social order, like
the theological order," reads the Preface to the cruelest of these
plays, *Le Prêtre de Némi,* "raises the question: who knows if
the truth may not be sad? The edifice of human society is built
upon a great void. We have dared to say this." [8] The world
seems given over to vanity, in the sense of futility and impotence,
in these dramas: the vanity of democracy in *Caliban,* the vanity
of science in *L'Eau de Jouvence,* the vanity of religious reform

in *Le Prêtre de Némi*—three faces of a single demon to be exorcised. A striking feature of all three plays is the effect they produce of a whirligig, a merry-go-round, of frustrated idealisms and triumphant *sottises;* recurrent images of the eternal circle, the wheel of fortune, the "endless comedy," the farce, re-enforce this impression.

Yet, as in the "comedy of history," reason is secretly at work achieving its ends in the "play of ideas." Despite moments approaching frenzied disillusionment, in both *dialogues* and *drames,* the total effect of both types of work is strangely tonic. The unique beauty of the *Dialogues* lies in the contrast between the content, which is often grim, and the form, which bespeaks calm, detached delight, as though their author were a dancing master exorcising ideas of terror by leading them through a gracefully organized ballet.[9] Over both dialogues and dramas, there presides the indestructible good humor of their author's robust spiritual nature rising above the most appalling manifestations of "poor humanity's" ineptitude.

The *drames* might equally well have been called *comédies,* for the comic gamut traversed is extremely wide. At its most poetic and sophisticated end, the delicate irony of Prospero. Close by, the irreverent wit of the Pope's mistress, Brunissende de Talleyrand ("Whoever drew a luckier ticket than you in the world's lottery? To be pope in an age of total corruption!"). Somewhere toward the middle, the assessments of what we like to call social and political order, by an astonishing parade of "men of good sense" and cynics. We have Orlando on the perpetual need for "heroes" as cannon-fodder ("Men are heroic only because they fail to reflect. So we must maintain a mass of idiots"); Voltinius on conservatism ("Every conservative once had a bandit for ancestor"); Metius on nationalism ("With the collection of virtues which make up what we call a great nation, one could compose the most detestable of individuals"); Leporinus's definition of military courage ("To run away forwards," *se sauver par devant,* killing all obstacles in the way); Ganeo's observation, as though he were commenting on the aftermath of World War II, that "a nation does better to be defeated in war. Woe be to the victorious nation! It becomes the slave of those who made it victorious."

Finally, at the opposite end of sophistication, there are the unconsciously comic effects thrown off by the platitudes and naive queries of all those anonymous "men of the people" and good "bourgeois" who act out the "endless comedy of human opinions." These rapid snatches of what Renan calls *conversations croisées* representing the voice of the people may well be the most original of his dramatic devices, anticipating to some extent the dialogue of a Beckett or a Ionesco. Yet if this is the equivalent of *le théâtre de l'absurde* in Renan, the sense of absurdity is totally without the twentieth-century sense of despair. The words of the Prieur des Chartreux, in *Caliban* (Act V, Scene 1), ring in our ears: the world is "a comedy composed of endless acts" (*une comédie composée d'actes sans fin*), but "At bottom, eternal reason is coming to light by the means that seem most to contradict it" (*Au fond, l'éternelle raison se fait jour par les moyens les plus opposés en apparence*).

VI   Assessment and Four Meanings of Play

The *Dialogues philosophiques* and *Drames philosophiques* are the culmination of a characteristic movement in Renan's thought, traceable, as I have shown, to some of his earliest pages, growing naturally out of his earlier works, and gaining strength as he matured: the tendency to view ideas in a context of play. Ranking with his greatest works, they are also among his most delightful, though they may be his most difficult to interpret. Without them, we would have a sadly truncated Renan.

The *Dialogues* are a highly original adaptation of Plato, who created the form, and of Plato's seventeenth-century imitator, Malebranche, admired since youth by Renan. The *Drames*, building upon a much less well-defined tradition—the "primitive model" of the *Book of Job;* Shakespeare's *Tempest, Coriolanus,* and *Julius Caesar;* Hugo's *Théâtre en liberté*—are a no less original achievement in the realm of what Renan calls *théâtre philosophique*.[10] Are they no more than mere "armchair theater"? Who can say with any confidence, knowing that plays by the greatest dramatists—Musset, Claudel, even Shakespeare—have been dismissed by critics as unfit for the stage, only to be produced triumphantly by the right director? I do not suggest that Renan is in a class with these playwrights, but merely that his disregard for the "petty demands" (*mesquines exigences*) of the conventional stage may, in our own age of brilliant successes in the theater of the "anti-theater," place at least the first three of his dramas in a more favorable light. Perhaps Renan awaits only a *metteur en scène* of genius.

The basic techniques of the play of ideas are two in number: development of an idea by showing its opposite; exaggeration of an idea either by playing down, or by omitting altogether, its opposite. These two methods are summed up in the following key sentences: (1) "A truly complete work should not need to be refuted by its reader. The opposite side of each thought should be indicated therein, so that the reader may seize at a single glance the two opposing faces of which every truth is composed" (Avant-Propos, *Le Prêtre de Némi*); (2) "The most forceful means of emphasizing the importance of an idea is to suppress it and to show what the world becomes without it" (Préface, *Dialogues philosophiques*). Both methods have been used in dialogues and dramas, creating the impression of a thinker who is testing his faith by confronting its denial, by acting the "devil's advocate" of his own most cherished beliefs. The "Jewish" Renan of *messianisme hébreu*, by which he meant "faith in the definitive triumph of religious and moral progress, the repeated victories of stupidity and evil notwithstanding" (Avant-Propos, *Le Prêtre de Némi*); the "Greek" Renan, "liberal" and "rationalist," whose confidence in the power of men to free themselves through knowledge and reason was continually battered but never destroyed—this optimistic Renan is conducting the amusing experiment of envisioning a world in which the love of virtue and truth have almost disappeared.

It was a dangerous game to play, since the reader unable to control these works by a knowledge of others in which Renan affirms his beliefs unambiguously, can be misled into concluding that the play of ideas is nothing more than an endless round of contradictions, an endless "coupling of antitheses and piling up of impossibilities" (as a voice in the crowd says, ridiculing the sibyll Carmenta). But Renan is writing for an élite, and this certainly includes those who know him well enough to understand that his harsh, his "sad" hypotheses are counterbalanced by more consoling ones.

The supreme achievement of Renan's philosophical dialogue and theater may lie in the marvelous variety of meanings he confers upon the concept of ideological play itself. (The French word, *jeu*, like the English word *play*, has several possible meanings.) These impressive ambiguities, almost as numerous as those contained in the "rich jewel case of synonyms" which he was proud of having discovered for God (*Nous avons trouvé à Dieu*

un riche écrin de synonymes, Avant-Propos, *Le Prêtre de Némi*),
may be summarized as follows:

1. Play as relaxation, sport, *divertissement*. Renan's explaining
this as the well earned compensation of an excessively serious
youth, as I have pointed out, tells only part of the story. The
truth is that by his lightness of touch in treating serious ideas,
he joins one of the oldest and most venerable of philosophical
traditions: the view of philosophy as a "noble game." [11] To accuse
him of juggling with ideas is thus to place him in the company
of Socrates and Plato.

2. Play as music. I have already referred to the "dance" or
"ballet" aspect of the *Dialogues philosophiques*. Certain scenes
of the *Drames*, on the other hand, are accompanied by music.
But much more significant than this is Renan's search for a form,
growing out of drama but surpassing it, which would express
more faithfully all the subtleties of his thought. We can only
speculate about the type of work he might have composed when
words finally failed him; he alludes to it only in passing: "Modern
philosophy will have its definitive expression in drama, or rather
in an opera; for music combined with the illusion of a lyrical
scene would serve admirably to continue thought, at the moment
when words no longer sufficed to express it" (Préface, *Collected
Dramas*). Who will set Renan to music?

3. Play as gamble. Though possessing his own beliefs about
the human condition, Renan was willing to admit the possibility
that other beliefs might be true. To speculate is to gamble on the
truth. "Gambling" metaphors, employed to describe various theories about the universe, abound in his works, but they are concentrated with special force in the *Drames*. Their climax is
reached in the great speech of Prospero, for whom the essence
of wisdom, given the uncertainty in which man must remain
concerning his destiny, is "to arrange it so that whatever hypothesis turns out to be true, one will not have been too absurd"
(*L'Eau de Jouvence*, Act III, Scene 2). Renan, quite frankly,
viewed his own faith in reason as a sublime gamble; he was prepared to admit that he might have placed the wrong bet. Before
accusing him of frivolity, one should remember that even Christian faith has been interpreted, and by some of its most austere
apologists (notably by Pascal), as a "noble wager."

4. Play as drama, as "comedy" in its etymological sense. This
aspect of the play of ideas, though perhaps the most obvious, is

also the richest in the number of ramifications to which it gives rise. Indeed, one of the chief sources of fascination in the *drames* is their author's skill in moving within them, and inviting us to interpret them, on several dramatic levels simultaneously. Life itself and history are "comedies." On their highest level, the battles take place in the realm of "pure idea" (or what Renan calls "ideal history"), devoid of local color or precision as to costumes and manners: "I beg someone kindly to tell me what century Prospero lived in" (Foreword to *Caliban*). Here, contrasts and oppositions are those of "absolute psychology": man the aristocrat versus man the democrat; tradition versus revolt; convention versus instinct; natural versus supernatural religion. But the settings are also vaguely historical (Némi and Alba Longa; Italy and France of the Renaissance; the French Revolution), disguising, in a manner not too difficult to penetrate, what are often specific conflicts of the Third French Republic of the late 1870's and the 1880's: popular versus authoritarian rule; anti-clericalism versus clericalism; France versus Germany; nationalism versus "the patriotism of humanity." [12]

On still another level, the personal, Renan's play of ideas as drama takes place in his own psyche. None of the characters speaks exclusively for Renan, and they all speak for him. Prospero and Antistius may be closest to his alter ego, but even the minor characters, even the women, mirror various aspects of his soul. One example among many: Pope Clement's mistress is described by an observer in almost precisely the same terms which Renan had used thirty years earlier, in *Essais de morale et de critique,* to qualify his ideal philosopher: "Her mockery is her way of taking possession of the universe: (*Sa raillerie est comme une prise de possession de l'univers*). But the most striking indirect self-portrayal may well be, curiously enough, the Abbess of Jouarre. Her mind is characterized as a "perfect harmony resulting from notes in opposition"; her "great intelligence" is credited with "grasping simultaneously the opposite poles of things." What more does the informed reader need to identify Renan's ideal self? The scholar's nobility which Renan chose as preferable to that of the ordained priest corresponds to the "nobility of the humblest mother," which replaces in Julie de Saint-Florent her "ancient royal rights" as abbess.

Why, if Renan's conscience were really so tranquil, he was still haunted, more than forty years after his religious crisis, by images of vows renounced, of a heretical priest (Antistius) re-

fusing to destroy his orthodox predecessor, is a question that a
literary psychoanalyst could best seek to answer. Perhaps the answer has nothing to do with a troubled conscience. Whatever the
case, in the extreme form taken by Julie's assertion of moral
freedom, in the face of death, Renan, not far removed from death
himself, has chosen a bold symbol to re-enact and justify anew
his own assertion of independence as a young man of twenty-two.
Julie's, "the approval of my inner oracle is all I need" (*L'approba-
tion de mon oracle intérieur me suffit*), could easily serve as an
epigraph for *Souvenirs d'enfance et de jeunesse*.

But there is an essential difference between the self-descrip-
tions, the oblique confessions of Renan in his play of ideas and
the self-portrait of his *Souvenirs*. In dialogues and dramas these
self-revelations, fragmentary and allusive, occasionally even
somewhat obscure and incoherent, must be pieced together to
form his *persona*. In the autobiography they have been arranged
into a polished and harmonious whole.

CHAPTER 8

Poetry of the Self

IN presenting to the public his autobiography—actually the
reminiscences of his childhood and youth down to his "first
steps outside Saint-Sulpice" at the age of twenty-two—Renan
was aware that the type of truth he was formulating for his
readers was less factual or historical than poetic in nature. He
makes this point clear early in the preface of the *Souvenirs d'enfance et de jeunesse* by linking the work with Goethe's great
autobiography, significantly entitled *Poetry and Truth* (*Dichtung
und Wahrheit*, 1811 ff.), and also by generalizing his own experience as an autobiographer into a striking maxim, put forward
as possessing universal truth: "What we say of ourselves is always poetry" (*Ce qu'on dit de soi est toujours poésie*).

I *Shaping One's Myth*

Poésie here, as with Goethe's *dichtung*, is synonymous with
"fiction," or what is imagined. To write one's life, for Renan, is
to "transmit to others the theory of the universe one bears within
oneself" (*transmettre aux autres la théorie de l'univers qu'on
porte en soi*). All that we have learned up to now of Renan leads
us to expect that such a "theory," or "system," as he also calls it,
though it may be based in part on scientific knowledge and organized in part according to rational logic, is nevertheless intended to convince us, in the end, by the kind of truth to which
we acquiesce in a well made, artistically credible poem or novel.
For what else is each man's metaphysics but his "epic poem on
the nature of things," his "novel of the infinite"?

Yet far from wishing to detract from the value of the *Souvenirs*
by calling attention to its "fictional" character, I merely recognize
the paradox that through fiction (never, one must add, purely
invented, but constantly mixed with or based on fact) Renan
expresses, as I shall illustrate later in more detail, a number of
truths about himself. He creates his own "myth"—and I use the
word in no negative or derogatory sense, but in the positive sense
in which, as a historian, he himself has used it: a people collec-

tively, in its myths, reveals better than in historical annals its true moral and spiritual being. The myth of the individual Renan is not unlike one of those collective myths to whose study he had given most of his life. The essence of his self is what he seeks to define in his *Souvenirs*, just as he had sought to define the essence of Christianity and Judaism in his historical work. The *Souvenirs* are the *Origines de Renan*, more specifically, *l'origine de mes jugements* (Préface, *Feuilles détachées*). Out of these images and reflections, "almost without order," he remarks in the Preface, which "came to my mind as I thus evoked a past old by fifty years," he creates his myth for posterity.

Once again, for all their differences in tone and method, Goethe, in this art of creating one's myth, was his master. A contemporary historian of religions, Mircea Eliade, who has done much to remind us of the positive value of myths and of the persistence of myth-making in modern cultures, points out that it is a "generally human" tendency to "transform an existence into a paradigm [i.e., model] and a historical personage into an archetype." "This tendency," he adds, "survives even in the most eminent representatives of the modern mentality. As Gide well perceived, Goethe was fully conscious of his mission to achieve an exemplary life for the rest of humanity. In everything he did, he strove to *create an example [créer un exemple].*" [1] Renan is one of those authors, like Goethe and Gide (one also thinks of Chateaubriand and Rousseau, and ultimately of Montaigne and Saint Augustine), who worked as assiduously at their lives as at their books and gave tireless care to shaping in print an ideal image of themselves worthy of surviving their mortal flesh.

The disposition to define his ideal self poetically dates as far back in Renan's career as his obsession with history and his propensity to the play of ideas. In the ninth volume of her edition of his complete works, Henriette Psichari has assembled, together with his *Cahiers* and *Lettres de famille*, the essential texts—the *Fragments romanesques* and *Ma Sœur Henriette*—which prepare the way for the definitive poem of the self, the Renan whole and harmonious, "sound in spirit and in heart" (*sain d'esprit et de cœur*) who is the protagonist of the *Souvenirs* and of their sequel, *Feuilles détachées*, published the year of his death in 1892. Diverse though these works are in their content and styles, unequal though they certainly are as artistic successes, they form a single thread in his production. They are so many attempts to resolve artistically the spiritual dilemmas around which his emotional life revolved: his attitude toward the female sex; his sense of guilt for the sacrifices he had imposed upon his sister; his need to justify the religious quality of his life as a free-thinking critic who had broken with Catholicism; his experience of suffering and anticipation of death; and, most important of all, the crucial problem for him subsuming all others, the challenge of harmonizing into a single whole the discordant notes of his existence.

II Early Poetic and Novelistic Fragments

Two works grouped by Madame Psichari with the *Fragments intimes et romanesques*, "L'Idéal" and "Evolutions déifiques de Pan," are poems dating from 1845. They are of interest, among other reasons, because apart from the many translations of Psalms embodied in his historical work, Renan wrote almost nothing in verse. Both poems consist of a series of unrhymed couplets with irregular verse lengths, varying from seven to as many as sixteen syllables, the majority being eight, nine, and ten syllables long. "Godlike Evolutions of Pan" is the slighter of the two pieces. Humanity speaks and, by means of succinct references to religious imagery, evokes in rapid succession some of its major religious beliefs (Judaism, e.g., in the lines, *Je me suis lamenté avec Israël, / J'ai appelé celui qui doit venir;* Christianity, in the lines, *J'ai vu Dieu dans un morceau de pain. / Ce Dieu-là se mange et se boit*). In the last few couplets humanity asserts its absolute freedom and self-mastery, its becoming at last a law unto itself, but hints at some ineffable mystery surrounding its struggle for impossible perfection (*Je lutte contre l'impossible, / Je maudis la langue des mortels*).[2] Like this poem, "L'Idéal," Renan tells us, stems from "the first moments in which I breathed free air." He was then, he adds, "filled with Hebrew poetry," and wrote these pieces "to make up for what I was unable to say in abstract language"—an allusion, quite probably, to the *Cahiers de jeunesse*.

In "L'Idéal" several motifs appear which will be worked out in greater detail in subsequent attempts, hereafter in prose, to define more satisfactorily the poetry of self: liberation from a state of slavery (orthodox Catholic faith) in which the poet was reduced to seeking his identity from passersby; the discovery that the individual soul alone is responsible for its "strength," "salvation," and "rank"; the nature of thought as a "bubbling cauldron," a chaotic, tumultuous plenitude which resists ordering and harmonizing; the vision of the opposite sex as a chaste, idealized woman, Béatrix ("One thinks not of her body in her presence"); the praise of suffering as a means of "touching God" ("Blessed be he who suffers"). Despite the boldness of the concluding couplet, "To feel and to think is the whole of man, / What he feels and thinks is his God," Renan is still too close to his childhood faith not to allow for some uncertainty as to whether his abnegation of it will bring him wisdom. The redemptive quality of suffering inevitably suggests the Saviour, as does the line evoking the Eucharist: "Ah! must God be concrete like bread?" (*Ah! faut-il qu'il soit concret comme du pain?*)

This conflict between intellect and heart, between the rational certainty of having acted rightly in renouncing his faith and the emotional uncertainty into which such a course of action plunges him, becomes even more intense in *Ernest et Béatrix*, the rough draft of a novel written in 1848. Vaguely imitative of two literary forms, already quite old-fashioned in 1848, namely the eighteenth-century epistolary novel and the Romantic *roman confession* centering around a young man's lyrical statement of his misfortune, this frail work (a mere fifteen pages in the Psichari edition) is the first of Renan's attempts to carry out a project already referred to in the *Cahiers:* the writing of "a novel completely about the psyche." [3] *Patrice* will follow close upon this as a second attempt. Only with the *Souvenirs,* begun almost thirty years later, will Renan finally perfect his technique of the *roman tout psychique,* thus in a sense beginning under the tutelage of Goethe's *Werther,* the true ancestor of the confessional novel, and ending under that of Goethe's *Dichtung und Wahrheit.* His explanation of why he wrote *Ernest et Béatrix,* in the work's Preface, could be applied not only to *Patrice* but also, astonishingly enough, to the *Souvenirs:* all three arise from what he calls a "commanding need . . . to express in a work adequate to my whole being the complete ensemble of my life," the need to reveal a side of himself other than "the philosophic and scientific side," in fact, "the deep-seated and intimate nature" of his life (*le fond, l'intime de ma vie*).

The Renan of twenty-five, still far from the master storyteller of the *Souvenirs,* admits taking few pains, in the abortive novel in name only that is *Ernest et Béatrix,* to translate his ideal self into imaginative terms. The barely existent "plot" tells of a young seminarian in the Paris of 1789 who is tormented by philosophical doubts as well as frustrated in his passion for a young Breton

girl who lives, as does his mother, in Tréguier; Ernest leaves the
seminary as Béatrix enters a convent; eventually the Revolution
causes her to return to the world; they are reunited briefly on
the island of Bréhat, off the Breton coast, but Béatrix resists
Ernest's love, and he is finally condemned to death by a revolutionary tribunal. Unsatisfactory though this fragment is as literary art, it has value as an outpouring of that "fullness of life"
which young Renan felt within him, which "sometimes reaches
intoxication, and which I cannot contain within the narrow
framework of learning."

The key to this work, as to *Patrice*, is the fact that Renan, in
his late twenties, had conquered his intellectual freedom but remained chaste. Intellectually, he may be mature; emotionally he
is still an adolescent. Ernest is his "ideal of human life, of perfection, of the man I would like to be"; but one essential thing
is lacking to make truly perfect his "harmony of all the elements
of humanity": sexual love. The most touching and charming feature of this imagined love story, awkwardly grafted onto the
document of a real religious crisis, is its curious theme of the
young man who "loves in general" and who has to create his own
"Béatrix," striving to make her as real as possible, as real as the
only women he has ever loved, his mother and his sister. The
poetry of the work lies not in its form but in its content, in the
vague indéfini of the author's heart, *thème éternel de toute poésie*,
and in the fierceness with which, like the Biblical wild ass of the
desert (*l'onagre*, to which he compares himself here as well as in
"Evolutions déifiques de Pan"), he cherishes the very liberation
from authority that has caused him to suffer by estranging him
from his loved ones in the faith. Sublimated sexual energy accom-
panies intellectual fervor in this crude, unfinished poem of the
self where no real harmony, no real dénouement can yet be
achieved, since its author still confesses preferring his heart to
his knowledge and his mind (*Je préfère mon cœur à ma science
et à mon esprit*).

In *Patrice*, written in Rome in 1849-1850, Renan returns to
grapple with the same problem that had beset him in *Ernest et
Béatrix*, the problem of the critically-minded and chaste youth
who, as Ernest had said, "envies the good fortune of those who
know only how to love," who questions his own ability to love
and laments his alienation from those who love out of simplicity
of heart. *Qua* novel, *Patrice* is incomplete and no more successful than the earlier fragment, possessing even less of a "fic-

tional" framework. From Rome on the eve of the French Revolution, Patrice writes to his beloved Cécile, who describes herself
as one of those naive young women "condemned to know only
the catechism and our prayers" (cf. Béatrix, only "half-believer,"
demi-croyante). What begins as an exchange of views, or epistolary dialogue, soon changes into a monologue in which Patrice
provides both a detailed account of his reactions to Rome and
a spiritual self-portrait.

But *Patrice* enjoys over *Ernest et Béatrix* at least two advantages tending to make it the more substantial of the two works.
First of all, its central theme is much more forcefully stated:
the contrast between the "harmony" of being, preserved by
Cécile in her simple faith, and the discord characterizing Patrice's
state of mind as an ex-believer. "For you," he tells her, "the
grand harmony is not disturbed; religion, duty, love, beauty
repose for you in a mystic and holy unity. You do not know the
struggle of the holy against the true, of the beautiful against the
good, of the true against itself." Secondly, *Patrice* is a much better constructed work than its predecessor. It has a dynamic
quality springing from the fact that the hero's thinking about
religion, under the impact of Rome, undergoes a change which
he describes as decisive in the "history of his inner life." (Here
Renan is recording quite faithfully his own reactions to Italian
Catholicism during his trip to Italy in 1849-1850.) What profoundly alters his attitude is his discovery that religion need not
be true in order to be beautiful. Here is a major step toward
recovery of his lost harmony of being. Catholicism he is now
able to view, with much greater equanimity than Ernest, as "our
mythology"; by accepting the artistic and even, to some extent,
the spiritual content of its symbols and myths, and leaving the
letter of doctrine to the devout (and he was not convinced that
devout Italians even took doctrine very seriously), he solved, in
some measure at least, the problem of "being Catholic, without
believing in Catholicism" (*N'y aurait-il pas quelque moyen d'être
catholique, sans croire au catholicisme?*).

Despite this change, however, Patrice is hardly, at the abrupt
end of his story, much nearer than Ernest to having recomposed
his ideal self in harmonious form. A comparison of *Patrice* with
Souvenirs d'enfance et de jeunesse is interesting from this point
of view. There is much, in this fragment of Renan's delayed
adolescence, that anticipates his mature self-portrait: the concern
to defend himself, as an apostate, in the eyes of orthodox be-

lievers (the opening section denying his pride, his *orgueil*, will have its counterpart in the apologetic note diffused throughout the *Souvenirs*); the glorification of his contradictions (*je me glorifie de mes contradictions*); the dualism marking those who, born into the Christian sense of the infinite, can never be wholly content with Greek "finiteness" and "measure." This last theme, preparing us distantly for the *Prière sur l'Acropole*, bears a strange resemblance to Rimbaud's complaint in *Une saison en enfer* of being "the slave of my baptism" (Patrice calls it "the misfortune of being born a Christian," *le malheur d'être né chrétien*). These are, in reality, two variations on a broader nine-teenth-century theme, the difficulty of being a true "pagan" (*païen*) in Catholic France.

III   *Harmony Disrupted*

But how far we still are from the poised, smiling reconcilia-tions of the *Souvenirs*, from that "healthful and finished work" (*une œuvre saine et achevée*) which Patrice, though the phrase is his, tends to consider impossible! In both sex and religion Patrice remains troubled, and it is obvious that his sexual and religious fears and uncertainties are distinctly related. His *timi-dité* is both the fear of destroying Cécile's purity as a woman and the fear of destroying the mystery of religious belief, for which she stands. Patrice's male voice of science and criticism jars discordantly with Cécile's female voice of natural instinct for poetry and faith. Out of this discord Renan will eventually fash-ion his harmonizing of these two voices of humanity, in "La Double prière" (*Feuilles détachées*).[4] Patrice, in the sharpness of wit with which he defends his position, has much more in him of the mature Renan than does the gushing Ernest, who is only one or two years younger. But Renan at twenty-six is still too pained by the suffering of having "ceased to be a child" to be able to exclude forever the possibility of a return to the Catholic faith. Here is another major difference between *Patrice* and the *Souvenirs*. The former still allows for an imagined reconver-sion;[5] the latter is also, in a real sense, motivated by a return to Catholicism, but with a wholly different purpose inspiring the author: that of letting his mind rest upon the beloved object of his childhood faith, while serenely and lucidly affirming his ir-reversible separation from it.

Patrice might have been subtitled *l'harmonie troublée* and the *Souvenirs*, *l'harmonie restaurée*. In between these two works

Renan composed another important exercise in extracting from
past experience the quintessence of an ideal self. This was *Ma
Sœur Henriette*, written in 1862, the year following his sister's
death, when he was almost forty, printed privately in the same
year, and published posthumously in 1895.

IV   *An Exemplary Life: Saint Henriette*

Ma Sœur Henriette relates, in chronological order, the life of
Henriette from the time of Ernest's first memories of her to her
death from malaria at the age of fifty, at Amschit during their
trip to Syria in 1861. Highlights of her biography, as Renan
presents it, are: her assuming responsibility for the family after
their father's death; the separations and reunions of brother and
sister; her role in obtaining an education for Ernest, serving as
confidante during his religious crisis, assisting in the launching
of his career, and collaborating with him as his *secrétaire*, his
"living index" (*index vivant*); the crisis of his marriage to Cornélie Scheffer, the uneasy *ménage à trois* that resulted, and the
transfer of her maternal affection (she never married or had
children) from her brother to her nephew, Ary; and, finally, their
last months together in the Middle East. This work might equally
well have been called *Ernest et Henriette*. It is clear that Henriette's reason for being, in her brother's eyes at least, is to serve
him, and that her life has little meaning apart from his. Nor does
Renan's inevitably biased interpretation really do violence to
what appears, concerning his sister, to have been the truth. Yet
—the problem will arise again for the *Souvenirs* and is therefore worth pointing out—by silences here, by exaggerations
there, Renan appears to contradict or distort a number of the
known facts. Had other witnesses told this story—the patient
Cornélie harassed by a jealous sister-in-law, or Berthelot, close
friend of Henriette, with whom he exchanged many a letter
complaining about Renan's egotism and lack of affection toward
both of them—the picture might have been somewhat different.
Its complexities and discords might have been less attenuated
(compare Renan's statement that there was no *note discordante*
in his sister's being); its harshnesses might have been less glossed
over.[6]

However, it is a moralist, artist, and poet in prose who is telling
the story, and his purpose is both quite simple and supremely
justified. *Ma Sœur Henriette* is a work of almost uniform eleva-

tion and purification. It is the life of a "chosen soul," a Christ-like figure. There are several references to her freely accepted "chalice" of moral suffering, and her ultimate physical suffering, while Renan, in moments of respite from his own grave illness, wrote his pages on the Passion and Last Supper, is bound to suggest the rapprochement with Christ. The book is, in fact, a "saint's life": "She was a saint, minus precise faith in a creed and narrow religious observances." All that is petty and commonplace has been removed, so that the central image, that of a woman courageously devoted to duty and ideal and exemplifying moral nobility without benefit of supernatural belief, may shine more brightly. The very vocabulary, with its accumulation and repetition of words like *devoir, âme, esprit, idéal,* and its noble circumlocutions, unrelentingly builds up this single effect of spiritual strength.

V *The Metaphysics of an Affection*

Had there been little or no basis in fact for this idealized portrait, had Henriette not been in reality a noble and tragic figure worthy of our admiration, this embellishment of her life in the neo-classical style would have been absurd. One point in its favor. Another is the great tact with which Renan, in a way that alone would make up for all his relatively minor inaccuracies, distortions, or subterfuges, casts his image of Henriette in terms that are faithful to her own manner of viewing things, her own esthetic. For just as she passed over concrete physical details, "local color," in order to extract from the landscapes and historical sites she observed their "soul," "idea," and "general impression," so Renan has concentrated fittingly upon her own spiritual essence as he conceived it. There is a sculptural quality about this work, not without a curious affinity to the Parnassian poetry of the 1860's. To "sculpt" verbally his sister's "moral personality" (the terms are Renan's) in such a way as to suggest something of the energetic will-power with which she herself "created her spiritual person"—this was Renan's goal, and in it there was no place for familiar anecdotes, touches of "realism," lengthy physical descriptions. Flaubert, who found the work disappointingly lacking in life-giving detail, was in this instance less perceptive than Charles Maurras, who admired it for its kinship with classicism and summed it up brilliantly as "the metaphysics of an affection" (*la métaphysique d'une affection*). In the epilogue Henriette is raised, in fact, to the power of a symbol ("All

here below is but symbol and image," *Tout n'est ici-bas que
symbole et qu'image*); the meaning of her existence, its endur-
ing and exemplary value, is firmly fixed as a "precious argument
for those eternal truths of which each virtuous life contributes
the proof." [7]

Ma Sœur Henriette, if read as one's introduction to Renan,
might seem like an unsuccessful attempt to revive the style of
the French classical funeral oration, à la Bossuet. Some experienced readers of Renan have found its devotional vocabulary,
even as adapted to the needs of free-thinkers, too reminiscent of
the precious, sentimental manner ridiculed in France as *le style
Saint-Sulpice.* The exaggerated refinements tend to cloy. Something of the artificiality permeating the whole work is present
from the very first paragraph, with its announcement that "these
pages are not written for the public, and will not be exposed
to it." (In fairness, though, one should add that Renan probably
meant "during my lifetime.") Would not the author have served
his sister's memory better by not turning her into a monument?

To such objections Renan might have replied by referring his
critics to a remark he had made in *L'Avenir de la science:* "I
prefer the affectation of the elevated to the banal" (*J'aime mieux
l'affectation de l'élevé que le banal*). Had he not even dared
paradoxically, in the same work, to defend the *précieux* against
Molière? But I think there is a more convincing way of showing
that *Ma Sœur Henriette,* though inferior to his *Souvenirs,* is none-
theless a kind of masterpiece. This strange book, liable to seem
so cold and affected on first reading, has the power to grow
upon the reader as he comes to know Renan better and to realize
that he wrote it not merely to fix the memory of his "noble and
tender friend," but also—perhaps above all—to exorcise the
"cruel thought" that haunted him, the thought of having been
responsible for her suffering. One comes to appreciate more
deeply the pathos which breaks through the highly stylized surface of the work, and to understand that beneath this surface
Renan is expiating a distinct sense of guilt. It is as though he
were asking pardon of Henriette now, saying now the *adieu* he
was unable to say when he himself lay unconscious next to his
dying sister, and consoling her by attributing to her—with an
exaggeration that can only be touching, if this is indeed its
motivation—his happiest hours and the most decisive influence
in shaping his own being.

Even the style comes to seem less abstract, more and more colored with true feeling, as one progresses in understanding of the work. Or the abstractness of the style as a whole serves to set off, in all the more striking contrast, a handful of unforgettable images: Henriette "playing dead" to tease Ernest as a child; sitting in her Breton shawl of green wool in the room adjacent to his study, the door ajar so as to see him at work; hastening to the Scheffers' to be reconciled with Cornélie whose marriage to Ernest she had almost succeeded in thwarting; communing long hours with him in conversation—the final joy before the final agony—on the terrace of their house in Amschit.

Renan came close, in this story of a brother who may have loved too little and a sister who loved "as one perhaps ought not to love" (*comme on ne doit peut-être pas aimer*), to writing his only tragic work.

VI *From Myth of Sister to Myth of Self*

The first chapter of what was to be *Souvenirs d'enfance et de jeunesse*, an episode entitled "Le Broyeur de lin" ("The Flax Grinder"), was written at Ischia in the fall of 1875 and first published in the *Revue des deux mondes* in March, 1876. Thus, almost thirteen years separate Renan's portrait of his sister and the earliest composed fragment of his self-portrait. The irony, humor, and comic spirit which permeate the *Souvenirs* are totally absent from *Ma Sœur Henriette;* nowhere in the margins of the latter would it have been appropriate for the author to write, as he was tempted to do on so many pages of the *Souvenirs,* "with a grain of salt" (*cum grano salis*). Renan's autobiography is the product of that hour in life, described in *Ma Sœur Henriette* as never striking for her, "when one gathers in what one has sown, when one sits down to remember past fatigues and sufferings." This hour clearly sounded for Renan, and he made the most of it. The gaiety, the irreverent wit which were an essential part of his makeup were lacking to hers; and, if we are to believe Renan, these gifts of his had been restrained, out of deference to her, in those works, including *Ma Sœur Henriette,* written in her shadow. In any case, suffering and sadness have been all but completely banished from the memory and imagination at work in the *Souvenirs.*

Nevertheless, the two books are very intimately related, and one is justified in including *Ma Sœur Henriette* among Renan's attempts to define his poetry of the self. Despite his statement that "one can never handle one's own biography in the same manner in which he treats that of others" (Preface, *Souvenirs*), Henriette was too much a part of himself for us not to suspect that in creating her "myth" he was continuing the process of perfecting his own. Renan tended to associate the *Souvenirs* in his own mind with the work which in its private printing had borne the subtitle *Souvenir pour ceux qui l'ont connue* (Memory for Those Who Have Known Her). It is significant that in the Preface to the *Souvenirs* he mentions having considered including his tribute to Henriette as part of his autobiography, adding that he excluded it finally because to do otherwise would have been "a kind of profanation," in a work very much "written for the public," like "exposing her portrait in an auction mart." A possibly unavowed reason for changing his mind may have been esthetic: this noble and melancholy figure would certainly have been an intruder in the humorous, and often outright comic, atmosphere of the *Souvenirs*. Perhaps Renan also divined, by deciding for posthumous publication of *Ma Sœur Henriette*, that his death, re-enforcing hers, would in some sense further consecrate his tribute to her and render its noble style less subject to ridicule.

The fact remains that *Ma Sœur Henriette* is in several curious ways a kind of sketch for the *Souvenirs*. If Henriette was a "living index" for Ernest's scholarly work, she was also, in those last days when she experienced "a kind of melancholy return to the past wherein all her family memories crisscrossed one another," a living source, thanks to which he could begin to recollect and meditate upon his own childhood and youth, in preparation for his far from melancholy return to the same past. In lifting her to "immortality" in the "conscience of humanity" (a Renanian synonym for God), he was giving careful thought to his own survival after death. Formulating her religious belief was another way of formulating his own: they shared the same ability to contemplate serenely "the distinction which every philosophic spirit is obliged to make between the essence of religion and its specific forms." To think of "rewards" for practicing virtue was beneath her, as beneath Renan's, dignity, for "virtue was not with her the fruit of a theory, but the result of an absolute habit of nature." To relate in detail how this *pli absolu de la nature* had been formed in himself is one of the major purposes of his *Souvenirs*. The tone, however, is immensely different: the noble style of *Saint Henriette* gives way to the unique blend of playfulness and seriousness more suited to a *Saint Renan.*

VII *Themes, Techniques, and Tones*

The principal themes of the *Souvenirs* are announced in the Preface, a piece of writing in itself, like most of Renan's prefaces, a well rounded and almost self-sufficient essay. His intention to sound the depths into which his faith has sunk, rescuing from his Catholic origins (*berceaux,* literally, cradles) what is of permanent value and disengaging lasting virtue from passing forms of supernaturalist dogma, is set forth in the lovely lyrical passage with which the Preface opens. He compares his lost faith to the legendary city of "Ys," buried in the Atlantic off the coast of Brittany, but still testifying to its existence by an occasional phantom sound of its cathedral bells when the sea is calm, an occasional vision even of its cathedral spires jutting up, when a storm rages, through the trough of a wave. A related theme is the concept of progress as taking its necessary point of departure in a "profound respect for the past." However radically he may seem to have broken with his ancestors' faith, Renan feels, as he will express it in a later chapter ("Mon Oncle Pierre"), that he "thinks for them" and that they "live in him" (*Je sens que je pense pour eux et qu'ils vivent en moi*).

Another motif introduced in the Preface, to be restated in many different forms in the body of the work, is the dualism of his nature. "Almost all of us are dual" (*Presque tous nous sommes doubles*), he writes, that is, composed of male insistence on intellect (development *par la tête*) and of female "irrationality" or trust in "instinctive being." Finally, just as Renan had transfigured Henriette's existence into a symbol of the validity of virtue and sacrifice, so he presents his drama of conscience as a symbol of the larger, universal drama: "the liberation of the human spirit" (*l'affranchissement de l'esprit humain*). And if the achievement of a young French seminarian in freeing himself from the error of dogmatic belief is but an image of humanity's struggle to attain the freedom of self-knowledge, this struggle in turn is part of something much vaster: nature's experiment —sure of succeeding, since it has the infinity of time and space in which to operate and can therefore make mistakes with impunity—in "the development of mind" (*le développement de l'esprit*).

Henriette, from her niche in the "conscience of humanity," would certainly have applauded most of this Preface; but it is very doubtful that her tastes would have been wide or flexible enough for her to appreciate the extraordinary diversity of styles, tones, and literary forms incorporated into the *Souvenirs*. Outside of Renan's best historical volumes, this may be the richest, most subtle, and most skilfully constructed of all his books. The work as a whole is built upon the contrast, also announced in the Preface, between the *récits de Bretagne* (chapters I and II, "impressions of child-like sensibility, candor, innocence, and love") and the *récits du séminaire* (chapters III-VI), dominated by "somber struggle, reasonings, and harsh scholasticism." But in each of these major divisions the techniques and tones are highly diversified. Lyrical passages alternate with passages of historical and philosophical reasoning and political observation; portraits of self, reminding one of little essays (the section on his "four virtues" in the last chapter even reads like an imitation of Montaigne), are fused with portraits of others, these last flowering at times into authentic short stories ("The Flax Grinder," "My Uncle Pierre," "Old Man System," "Little Noémi"). Renan's poetry of self is inseparable from the fictional process by means of which he brings others back to life. The descriptions and tales of Breton eccentrics, "madmen" (*fous*), and saints are designed to reveal traits which the autobiographer shares: propensity to dreams; the understanding of love as delicately spiritualized feeling rather than passion; a will-power energetic enough to maintain, against terrible odds, one's chosen ideal or accepted duty.

Nor does Renan fail to exploit the dramatic quality of his story. By this I refer not only to the dramatic touches of individual scenes, such as Talleyrand's deathbed conversion by Dupanloup (a masterpiece of comic irony), or the climactic moment when Abbé Gottofrey, vibrating with excitement, tells Renan, "You are not a Christian!" (*Vous n'êtes pas chrétien!*), or the very touching scene in which his mother, during one of their accustomed walks together, seated with him "in the valley of the Guindy, near the chapel of the Cinq-Plaies, beside the spring," guessing all without fully understanding, tore from his hands the learned book she suspected was the enemy of her most cherished thought: to see her son a priest. I refer also, in fact above all, to the movement of the work as a whole. There is a certain dramatic power inherent in the fundamental theme itself, as stated

by Renan: "the reconciliation of the religious spirit, in its highest
form, with the critical spirit" (*la conciliation de l'esprit haute-
ment religieux avec l'esprit critique*). Knowing what the dénouement will be before it takes place still does not deprive us of
the suspense of the how and the why.

Dramatic, then, the *Souvenirs*, but hardly tragic. "All's well
that ends well" (*Tout est bien qui finit bien*), the author reminds
us. His greatest tour de force is to have turned his "somber struggle" into a comic masterpiece without sacrificing the seriousness
of his image. All the qualities he includes in the mock-solemn,
learned term *eutrapélie* (from the Greek, *eutrapelia,* the disposition to joke in a pleasant manner)—a "lively taste for the universe" (*un goût vif de l'univers*), "the pleasure of living and
creating" (*le plaisir de vivre et de produire*), the unassailable
sense of playful wit and *blague*—tend to give the book, especially
in its final chapter, its strongly comic coloration. "After sixty
years of serious life, one has the right to smile: and where is
there a more abundant source of laughter, closer to hand and
more inoffensive, than in oneself? If ever a comic author wished
to amuse the public with my foibles (*mes ridicules*), I would
ask of him only one thing, to take me as his collaborator . . ." In
the *Souvenirs,* Renan is his own comic co-author.

VIII   *The Truth of Fiction: Lineaments of a Self-Portrait*

Diverse though the tonalities of the book are, and meandering
though its narrative flow may sometimes appear to be, the essential components of Renan's ideal self emerge firmly and clearly
from the whole. I offer the following outline of his self-portrait,
pointing out in what respects (and suggesting for what reasons)
he has chosen to sacrifice the literal to the poetic truth.

1. *Disinterestedness, impracticality, spectatorship.*

Renan delights in imagining himself as the impractical
dreamer, the scholar full of timidity and *gaucherie,* a traveller
barely capable of making his way about in Parisian omnibuses
(*voyageur sans sérieux*), who, had not some special providence
looked after him, might not have survived at all in the world.
Such an image is hard to reconcile with the facts of the successful academician, the organizer of learned missions and other
learned enterprises, the administrator of the Collège de France.
Nor does the picture of the pure spectator thanking the "cause

of all good" for his delightful *promenade* across the most amusing of centuries quite fit with what we know of the political
writer and political candidate, concerned, often to the point of
prophetic zeal, with the criticism and reform of his age. Why
has Renan played down the practical side of his nature? For
two reasons, I think: because he felt that the joys of scholarly
contemplation were really more lasting than whatever satisfac-
tions political intervention might bring him; and because both
as seminarian and as political philosopher he had been "deceived," first by the Christian God and then by contemporary
events. To have wished, purely as a protective device, to min-
imize his potential for action and to give the appearance of
affirming less than he really believed, was hardly reprehensible
on his part, although it has undoubtedly lowered his standing
as an *écrivain engagé*.

2. Un-literaryness.

That this meticulous artist in words should affirm himself to be
"the least literary of men" (*le moins littéraire des hommes*) is, at
first glance, the most puzzling of his self-interpretations. Yet
how could we expect Renan—influenced as he was by a whole
line of austere prose writers, from the seventeenth-century authors of Port-Royal down to Henriette and the Jansenist editor
of the *Journal des débats,* Sacy, and trained as he was to view
style as strictly the instrument of thought—ever to have overcome completely his suspicion that literary art is somehow a sin,
or at best a fault to be palliated by concealing one's literary
efforts? His preoccupation with the problem of "sincerity" shows
that he is a post-Romantic, for this problem hardly existed before
Romanticism; his manner of solving it, by asserting that true
honnêteté littéraire must lie in "complete forgetfulness of form,"
proves a certain kinship with Classicism. The pages of the *Souvenirs* devoted to his ideal of style seem less to reflect his actual
practice than to constitute an interesting attempt to reconcile the
littérateur in himself with the thinker and to preserve for the
writer, in the midst of his literary fame, the illusion that his work
is not without naturalness and spontaneity.[8] Thus, what is probably the most highly polished piece of prose he wrote, the *Prière
sur l'Acropole,* he imagines as a prayer which he composed "on
the Acropolis, when I had succeeded in understanding its perfect beauty," and which, having found it among some old papers
remaining from his travel notes, he now presents to the public.

The prosaic truth, on the contrary, seems to be that the *Prière* was merely conceived and sketched in Athens in 1865 and completed some eleven years later, in 1876.[9] But who will be severe with Renan for this little mystification, when it reveals so much to us about his literary ideal?

3. *Serenity of conscience.*

"My peace of mind is perfect" (*Ma paix d'esprit est parfaite*). This attitude by no means dates from the *Souvenirs*. In letters written shortly after the resolution of his religious crisis, as well as in *L'Avenir de la science*, we find evidence that Renan achieved this peace of mind early in his career. "I wish to all my brethren remaining in orthodoxy a peace comparable to that in which I live now that my struggle has ended and that the calm following the storm has left me in the midst of this great tranquil ocean, a sea without waves or shores, where one has no other star but one's reason, no other compass but one's heart" (*L'Avenir de la science*). In "La Poésie des races celtiques" (*Essais de morale et de critique*) he had described *l'aimable sérénité de la conscience celtique*, tracing it to the Celtic tendency to regard evil as a "fact of fatality" rather than "a product of human conscience"; he had attributed to Saint Brendan, and had claimed for his own, the ideal of "the world seen through the crystal of a stainless conscience . . . a human nature such as Pelagius wished it, without sin." (The blend of documentary history and poetry, of *fiction* and *réalité* in that great essay is curiously anticipatory of the whole *Souvenirs*.)

What is new, and highly original, in the *Souvenirs* is his reversal of the traditional autobiography (Saint Augustine, Rousseau) wherein the author confesses his faults and champions the new way of life to which he is committed. Renan confesses instead his "four clerical virtues": disinterestedness (or "poverty of spirit"), modesty, politeness, and the avoidance of close friendships. Nothing here of those spiritual frustrations, of that laying bare of a troubled soul, which one might have expected of the fugitive seminarian; no harsh memories, retroactive hostility, or anti-clericalism. And when he does recognize his faults—being a "failed priest" (*prêtre manqué*) and having given way too easily to the *petit carillon* of his literary talent—his *mea culpa* is swathed in the same delightful irony as his catalogue of virtues. "One succeeds above all by one's faults" (*On réussit surtout par ses défauts*). By dwelling playfully on his virtues and satis-

faction with self, Renan thwarts the "secret designs" of a vanity
which leads most autobiographers to confess their sins in the
hope of acquiring "by ricochet great merits" (*par ricochet de
grandes qualités*). "He who despises himself nevertheless esteems
himself as despiser," wrote Nietzsche. Whatever other forms of
self-deception Renan may have succumbed to, he is refreshingly
free from this one.

4. *Gaiety*.

In his poetic image of self, Renan has greatly attenuated his
suffering. "I have never suffered very much" (*Je n'ai jamais
beaucoup souffert*). Even allowing for the qualifying *beaucoup*,
this seems to contradict flatly the extensive evidence provided in
writings contemporaneous with his religious crisis that he not
only experienced moral suffering but also prized it highly, in
somewhat Romantic fashion, as the mark of a privileged being.[10]
And what of his acute physical distress, his premature old age
in which hardly a day passed without intense rheumatic pain?
The answer, I think, so far as physical suffering is concerned,
is that he *willed* not to recognize it, thereby rising above it. As
for moral suffering, it too was very real, but he was able to
dominate this also, by drawing upon the rich resources of a
gaieté which he rightly describes as "the basis of my character"
(*le fond de mon caractère*). Thanks to his having tended and
nourished this *gaieté*—the product of the ancient race to which
he belonged and an inheritance, he remarks with paradoxical
humor, that one had to work hard to preserve—suffering did, in
fact, merely disturb the surface of his life.

5. *Unity reconciling dualisms and contradictions*.

Renan views himself as *l'homme double*, comparable to the
hircocerf of medieval Scholastic myth, part goat and part stag
(Prospero in *L'Eau de Jouvence* is also referred to in this manner). He unfolds freely and accepts calmly the many forms of
dualism to which his racial and cultural inheritance made him
subject: idealistic Breton versus mocking Gascon; Romantic
in "soul" and "imagination" (*romantisme moral*) versus non-
Romantic in form; dreamer and madman versus bourgeois; political utopian versus political realist; rationalist versus irrationalist.

The most important variation on the rich theme of Renanian
duality is the *Prière sur l'Acropole*, a statement in poetic prose

of how the Celt in Renan, incurably dreaming of the infinite, is unable fully to accept the Greek ideal of reason and finite perfection. Although the sheer verbal beauty of this sensuous, sonorous invocation to the Goddess Athena is not hard to appreciate, the reader is likely to feel its spiritual force only after further initiation into Renan and many rereadings. In the most thorough study to date of its genesis, background, sources, manuscripts, and definitive text, Henriette Psichari has shown it to be, not, as most critics have prematurely claimed, "a grand lyrical tirade, a kind of artificial prose poem, intended for recitation on a stage," but rather, a carefully planned and incredibly rich expression of one of Renan's dominant ideas (what she calls *une idée maîtresse de la pensée renanienne*), namely, the confrontation within himself, without torment, of the conflicting Celto-Christian and Greek ideals.[11]

IX *Harmony Restored*

To detach the *Prière sur l'Acropole* completely from the context of the *Souvenirs* as a whole, as many have done, is a mistake. It is best understood as a poem within the larger poem, a mythical fragment of the larger myth of self. Though a detail of microcosmic value in reflecting the author's spiritual world, it is, like all the other details, subordinated to his overriding aim in the *Souvenirs:* to justify the vision of his life as unity, continuity, and harmony. The *Souvenirs* is Renan's definitive expression of his conviction—his reasoned and coherent illusion, if one will—that within himself there has been no violent break with either his Breton or his Catholic heritage and that he has preserved intact the essence of this dual tradition. The concluding sentences of *La Prière sur l'Acropole* read: "The faith one has had must never be a chain. We have done our duty toward it when we have wrapped it carefully in the purple shroud wherein sleep the dead gods." Patrice had still felt himself to be somehow the captive of the faith he had given up; the mature Renan, having respectfully buried faith as an absolute and kept alive what is relatively true in faith as moral teaching, feels no "subjugation" whatever (no *assujettissement*) to the past.

I referred earlier to the delicately comic spirit which seems to me to preside over the *Souvenirs*. Nowhere does it appear more delightfully than at the point where Renan reaches what is the central argument in his attempt to establish the unity and

continuity of his life: his claim that he owed to the priests who
educated him the very love of learning and truth that had made
him free.[12] The "paradoxical wager" he has carried off is to have
"maintained clerical virtues, without the faith which serves as
their basis and in a world for which they are not made. . . ."
Renan the free-thinker thus transforms himself into the prize
pupil of Saint-Sulpice. That he appreciated the comic essence
of this argument is clear from the context, for the remark about
his *gageure paradoxale* is part of the passage, quoted earlier in
this chapter, calling for a "comic author" to assist him in telling
his story.

Yet the comic irony envelopes serious truths. Elsewhere in the
Souvenirs Renan had gone so far as to declare, in words this
time with no salt of humor in them, that the "spirit of Saint-
Sulpice" had provided him with "the profoundest law of my
entire intellectual and moral development." At best this would
seem, like the somewhat too decisive role he had assigned to
Henriette in his formation, to be an exaggeration. Like all the
other distortions of his factual record—the emphasis on disinterestedness, the "forgetfulness of form," the attenuation of suffering
and struggle—this forging of a too solid link with his ecclesiastical teachers is not so much error as oversimplification in the
interests of poetic truth. Henry James concluded his discriminat-
ing review of Renan's *Souvenirs* with these words: "Even his
affectations are illuminating, for they are either exaggerations
of generosity or ingenuities of resignation." [13]

X *Between Classical and Modern Autobiography*

To his superb achievements as historian, essayist, and philosophical dialogist and dramatist, Renan deserves to add a final
title to distinction: his conquest of autobiography. His *Souvenirs
d'enfance et de jeunesse* ranks high among masterpieces in a
field where they are rare. In *Feuilles détachées*, a collection of
essays and speeches intended as the sequel to the *Souvenirs,*
Renan speaks of his "great joy in rediscovering old memories"
(*ma grande joie est de retrouver d'anciens souvenirs*).[14] Few
authors have so successfully translated their own joyful return
to the past into pleasure for their readers. But the *Souvenirs* is
much more than great entertainment. It is the culmination of
a series of efforts, dating back to his youth, to define his poetic
image of self, to do justice to the "exquisite novel" (*le roman*

exquis) of his life, counteracting, with a legend of his own creation, the false legends, the malicious "apocryphal texts" already
beginning to circulate during his lifetime (Préface, *Feuilles détachées*). In the *Souvenirs*, he has, as Yeats said of his friend,
W. E. Henley, managed "to bring life to the dramatic crisis and
expression to that point of artifice where the true self could find
its tongue." [15] Only Renan had the subtle power to tell us what
irony and what happiness were attached to his being a *prêtre
manqué*.

The British critic, Roy Pascal, in one of the finest studies of
the genre of autobiography, refers in passing to Renan, along
with De Quincey, Stefan Zweig, and Somerset Maugham, as an
exemplar of a new, post-classical type of autobiography, the
"essayistic," in which "personal circumstances are used as the
basis for reflections on contingent matters." [16] This critic, for
whom autobiography "reveals as inexorably as poetry the quality
of the soul," tends to judge all works in the genre in the light of
classical autobiography; his thesis is that achieving the view of
one's life as a coherent whole has become increasingly difficult
in an age when men are less and less sure of their identity. Yet,
the more one reflects on his exacting criteria for great autobiography, the more one feels justified in claiming that Renan
has satisfied almost all of them, thereby deserving a place higher
than that of a French Somerset Maugham, let us say closer to
that of the writer who in fact inspired him (and whose concept
of autobiography is also one of Roy Pascal's major touchstones
of greatness); namely, Goethe.

How do these criteria apply to Renan? He seeks less to un-
cover the past for its own sake than to use it to reveal (in his
case, to justify) his present position, organizing the past in his
imagination and bringing it into balance with the present. By
avoiding what Roy Pascal calls the "annals" of a life, in favor
of its "philosophical history," by eschewing "continuous narrative
event" in favor of limiting himself to "significant relationship"
(concentration on the pivotal role played by his religious crisis),
Renan is able to achieve "a coherent shaping of the past." How
can it be fair to censure him for distorting some of the facts,
when "too scrupulous an adherence to the factual truth" may
harm rather than strengthen an autobiography or when "the
distortions of the truth belong to the values of autobiography
and are as revealing as the truth"? Finally, by capturing the
essence of what he willed to be, his "daemon," "persona," or

"life illusion," Renan attains what Roy Pascal calls "the distinction of great autobiography . . . not so much the truth of knowing as the truth of being." In only one important respect does
Renan seem to me to be lacking, in terms of this critic's criteria:
if the reflection of change is indeed essential to successful autobiography, Renan runs counter to this in his determination to
show his changelessness.

Renan the autobiographer may be "classical" in still a further
sense, as defined by the author of *Design and Truth in Autobiography*. There is, in his *Souvenirs,* no real hesitation as to
his destiny, no significant questioning (compare the more mod-
ernistic Stendhal) of who or what he is. The poem of his life
has the classical quality of being ripened and perfected; it is a
calm fulfillment, with no further "surprises" (*je n'ai rien réservé
pour personne*); it has none of Yeats' feeling that all he had
done or been was somehow a preparation for something else to
come. Profoundly classical also is the wisdom, the *sagesse,* with
which Renan faced the end of his life. We remember that Marcus
Aurelius (as well as Goethe) was his master in this genre. "Let
us enjoy the remainder of what is granted to us. We have had
our five acts, and, as Marcus Aurelius said, 'he who dismisses
us is without anger'." Like the ancients, Renan had a "kind of
religious respect for the spectacle of a happy life" ("Réponse à
M. Clarétie," *Feuilles détachées*).

Nevertheless, for all his classical qualities, accuracy may demand that we place Renan somewhere between the classical and
the modern autobiographies. Although he has sketched his spiritual portrait with firmness, he has allowed some uncertainties,
some vaguely troubling contradictions, to remain unresolved.
Thus, in striking contrast to the virtual elimination of suffering
in the text of the work, he has added an Appendix of letters
to fellow seminarians, Liart and Cognat (1845-1846), which contain distinct references to his *souffrance.* (Despite his having
censored these in curious ways, as Professor Pommier has shown,
he permitted this irrefutable proof of his suffering to stand.)
And do not the references to damnation and blasphemy in the
last pages of the text also cast slight shadows—whether or not
this was the author's intention—over the determined gaiety? His
viewpoint may be, on the whole, serenely classical, but out of
the corner of his eye he seems to glimpse distant disasters in the
making: "The whole of Europe has been attacked by some profound sickness" (*l'Europe entière est travaillée de quelque mal*

profond). The solid texture of the work, its marvelous equilibrium, succeed nevertheless in conveying the impression of something fragile, with the fragility of a life in which only firmly
willed devotion to duty, only stubborn fidelity to one's inner
oracle and maintenance of one's private ethic, prevent collapse
into frivolity or nihilism. "I persist in believing that existence is
the most frivolous thing in the world, unless one conceives of it
as a great and continual duty."

It is not my intention to offer these remarks as negative criti-
cisms. On the contrary, the ultimate stroke of genius on the part
of Renan, "poet of the self," may be to have succeeded in
defining the essential features of his nature as he willed them
into being and wished them to be remembered, while managing
at the same time to remain something of an enigma. He has
not—and we should be grateful for this—told all. "The apparent
reserve of the Celtic peoples," he wrote in *La Poésie des races
celtiques*, "which is often mistaken for coldness, may be explained by that inner timidity which causes them to believe that
a feeling loses half its value when it is expressed, and that the
heart should have no other spectator than itself (*le cœur ne doit
avoir d'autre spectateur que lui-même*)." Renan's poetry of the
self preserves, in the last analysis, more than a touch of the
mystery we have come to expect of all great poetry.

CHAPTER 9

A Harmony of Discords

RENAN was a great experimenter in the bringing together of opposites, of apparent irreconcilables: "One must be a mystic with factual certainty and the scientific method" (*Il faut être mystique avec le positif et la méthode scientifique); nous sommes dogmatiques critiques;* "God is both being and becoming"; "the unfathomable depth our father" (*l'abîme notre père*); "I have criticized everything, and, whatever is said, I have maintained everything" (*J'ai tout critiqué, et, quoi qu'on en dise, j'ai tout maintenu*). But to state these contradictions is merely the first step toward grasping his meaning. Many critics go no further, in fact blind themselves against seeing further. The illusion they have of Renan—a comfortable illusion, excusing them from probing more deeply into his purpose or being stimulated or disturbed by his thought—is that of a writer who cannot make up his mind, who has nothing to give us but irresolution. Even friendly critics tend to repeat complacently their short-sighted view of him as a thinker who merely takes pleasure in contradictions.

I *Variations on the Central Theme*

To do justice to Renan one must take a further step and recognize that his real purpose is to create a higher harmony of discords, like some composer of a new intellectual music of dissonances. The central theme of Renan's work, as of his life, is his attempt to create what Romain Rolland calls *une harmonie de contradictoires*.[1] This theme runs like a strong thread through all his writings:

The life of humanity, like the life of the individual, rests upon necessary contradictions. (*L'Avenir de la science*)

Criticism consists in maintaining contradictory elements opposite each other, in not letting a single component of humanity stifle any other. (*Patrice*)

The life of nations, like that of individuals, is a compromise between contradictions. (*La Réforme intellectuelle et morale*)

It was [the Abbess of Jouarre's mind] like a perfect accord resulting from opposing notes, the philosophy of our time and the love of
the past blended and pacified. (*L'Abbesse de Jouarre*)

All its [the world's] dissonances blend, at a certain height, into a
supreme harmony, which is love. (*Feuilles détachées*)

As temperament, as stylist, as political thinker, and as philosopher, Renan sought above all to blend opposites.

If the world was for him a marvelous spectacle, his own mind,
in its ability to see "the two sides of which every truth is composed," is no less marvelous a spectacle for his readers. Sensitive
to tradition, to values worth preserving though centuries old, he
nevertheless has a very modern faith in the scientific outlook.
His willingness to believe that the world may be an illusion, or
what Shakespeare calls an "insubstantial pageant," in no way
lessens his delight in savoring the vision, his zeal in pursuing
the truth and in changing the world for the better. Spectatorship
and participation, detachment and political action, are equally
important to him. His critical spirit does not exclude a certain
intellectual passion. He is that rare phenomenon: the critic who
is also a creative artist.

As a stylist he is great for the perfectly rhythmic and perfectly
euphonious sentences that flow with such ease (at least the
reader has this illusion), with such fertility from his pen. Of
Lamennais: *Le repos lui fut refusé ici-bas: d'impatience en impatience, il arriva jusqu' à la mort, toujours déçu par la noble
inquiétude de son cœur. . . . Il se coucha dans son obstination,
devenue raisonnée, et mourut dans sa colère.* His images, though
much less abundant and varied than those of Balzac or Montaigne, seem, like theirs, to rise like lucky discoveries (*trouvailles,*
the French say), without the tense or belabored approach of
Flaubert. Of Lombardian feudalism he writes that "the people
could breathe more easily through the pores of these discon-
tinuous masses" (*le peuple pouvait plus facilement respirer par
les pores de ces masses disjointes*).

But the true power of his style lies in its harmonizing of
opposites. He questions searchingly the limitations imposed upon
fullness of expression by the classical tradition of elegance,
clarity, and regularity in prose; at the same time he chooses to

work within these "precious limits" and to exploit the secret
power of classical style to express thoughts foreign to itself. Just
as he speaks the language of priests, but with a different meaning, so he speaks the language of classical French, but with much
more feeling for the polychromatic or polyphonic nature of truth,
for its elusiveness and approximateness, than we find in Descartes, Voltaire, or even in his much-admired Fénelon. His style
manages to convey the effects both of "French lightness" (*légèreté française*) and "Breton stubbornness" (*opiniâtreté bretonne*); a thought which is at once fleeting and decisive, playful
and yet firm in its hold upon a world that is serious and is to
be judged in the light of an ideal. Irony, though by no means
his only important tone, may be his greatest and most characteristic way of reconciling opposites. "Style in prose or verse,"
wrote Robert Frost, "is that which indicates how the writer takes
himself and what he is saying. . . . Many sensitive natures have
plainly shown by their style that they took themselves lightly in
self-defense. They are the ironists." [2] Renan remains one of the
supreme ironists of literature.

Politically, the discordant notes which Renan attempts to harmonize are, on the one hand, the order, purpose, and excellence
he associated with aristocratic or authoritarian rule, and, on the
other, the freedom and enlightenment of the many which republican or democratic rule, hopefully, would provide. He may well
have been, as Gaston Strauss claimed, an aristocrat by sympathy
and a democrat by necessity. But I prefer to phrase the matter
in more philosophical terms. Renan raised, but could not answer,
the basic question: are order, purpose, and excellence compatible
with democracy? He vacillates between faith in the tradition of
democratic enlightenment and the inclination to agree with the
older Stoic belief that only a small élite possesses wisdom and
that the masses are probably uneducable. (Like so many nineteenth-century thinkers, he was greatly influenced by the revival
of Stoicism.) Though we may not like this vacillation, we must
admit that he faced the issue squarely. An aristocrat by taste
and a proponent of the autocratic élite by theory, his life-long
role in popularizing so many historical and philosophical discoveries of his age gives him the right to be considered, in a
very real sense (the point is usually overlooked), a friend of
democracy. This great *vulgarisateur*, for all his theoretical skepticism concerning political enlightenment, is in practice a gener-

ous provider of the cultural enlightenment which is a precondition of political democracy.

The harmonizing of discords in the realm of religious philosophy he undoubtedly considered his most difficult challenge. His goal was clear and praiseworthy: to reconcile religion and reason. The author of *Les Apôtres* echoes Patrice: "Nothing should reign on this earth to the exclusion of its contrary; no one force should be allowed to suppress the others. The harmony of humanity results from the free emission of the most discordant notes. . . . Lucretius and Saint Theresa, Aristophanes and Socrates, Voltaire and Francis of Assisi, Raphael and Vincent de Paul, have equal reason for being, and humanity would be less great if a single one of the elements composing it were lacking." A noble statement. But the major weakness of Renan's thought is to have remained too much under the shadow of his Christian past, too much in bondage to Christian ways of thinking. A successful rebel against Catholic orthodoxy in his youth, he never succeded in breaking cleanly with Christianity. I do not doubt his sincerity in holding that the joys of the Christian believer are as nothing compared to the joys of the scholar in pursuit of truth and beauty. I recognize and admire his strength in resisting a return to formal Christianity. But the supernatural beliefs which he banished from the front door of his thought merely returned through the back.

Renan's inability to shake off completely his longing for personal immortality and for a personal God—"someone," as Antistius puts it, "to whom to address an actor's aside, a universe with two in it, where man establishes a conversation with the absolute on comradely terms"— must be considered a failing of his thought, though one which gives surprising pathos to his work. How much greater his humanism would have been had he not been compelled to believe that "a world without God is horrible" (Théoctiste, *Rêves*), had he not been so reluctant to abandon the postulate that individual immortality alone gives purpose to life. What extraordinary unity there is in this existence wherein "Ernest" (*Ernest et Béatrix*) predicts, Prospero reiterates, and Renan on his deathbed finally affirms a death "in the communion of humanity and of the Church of the future" (*Je meurs dans la communion de l'humanité et de l'Eglise de l'avenir*)![3] And yet Renan's Church of the future suspiciously resembles the church of the past; his religion of humanity, a Christianity shorn of everything except its moral code. His *divin,*

his *Eternel* has too many features of God the Father. His long
voyage from Grace to Nature, as Pommier so beautifully terms
it, was in reality never completed.

One would be tempted to call this Renan's only illusion, and
to tax him with self-deception, had not he been the first to admit
that he was the willing dupe of a hidden God, an incurable
chrétien de sentiment. With lucidity, with calm though ironic
regret, he confessed that his ethics, in the end, were impossible
without some vestige of a Christian belief already grown quite
insubstantial even among modern Christians. "We live on the
shade of a shade. On what will one live after us?" (*Nous vivons
de l'ombre d'une ombre. De quoi vivra-t-on après nous?—Préface,
Feuilles détachées*).

Renan saw the need for a new morality but failed to develop
it. In the history of Western thought he stands between the
Hegelian world of reason and of the absolute, and the Nietzschean
world of revolt and nihilism leading to a positive morality without God. Greek, Stoic, and Judeo-Christian traditions of a transcendent goodness and justice still have meaning for him and
bolster his position; but he is assaulted by doubts of a more
modern nature, and glimpses a world that may be inscrutable,
irrational, even absurd. He stands on the threshold of the
twentieth century.

II *A Natural Canonization*

An important facet of Renan's harmony of discords has thus
become outdated: his attempt—one of the last and most valiant
on the part of a major writer—to base an ethic largely on Christianity without believing in its supernatural teachings. But once
the weakness of his religious thought has been recognized, more
than enough remains in his work and in the example of his life
to make him a living presence. He is that rare creature, a great
scholar who is also a great writer, communicating his learning,
with art and imagination, to the common reader. His purely
scholarly activities alone would have filled a lifetime and left
their mark. But he was more than an extremely learned man.
"His originality," writes René Dussaud, "is to have carried his
combined gifts of philologist and historian into a realm until
then reserved for theologians, that of the history of religions,
and to have annexed this discipline to history properly speaking." [4] The courage with which he resolved his religious crisis
as a young man, and the courage with which he voiced unpopu-

lar truths, especially political truths, as a mature writer, provide a lesson for a world in which the very notion of conscience is being eroded, daily, hourly, by the pseudo-values of conformism, prestige, and the manipulation of image. Renan is a powerful reminder that conscience exists.

He is also a welcome antidote to despair. One turns to him, as to Montaigne and Voltaire, when one tires of the tragic sense, of absurdity, of fatalism, and of the glandular approach to life's problems. His wit and intelligence, among the keenest in literature, are all the more satisfying because they do not stifle his poetic imagination. Nor does his lucid awareness of human folly, of human limitations, ever destroy his faith in the human potential for truth and for good. The time has come to refute once and for all the myth that his skepticism discourages, debilitates, paralyzes. On the contrary, never total, and qualified by a minimum of certitudes, it is tonic. It stands as a reproach to our age of renewed fanaticism.

"Death cancels everything but truth," wrote William Hazlitt, "and strips a man of everything but genius and virtue. It is a sort of natural canonization." [5]

In this sense, it is not so ridiculous after all to call him "Saint Renan."

Notes and References

Chapter One

1. The present chapter is based largely on Renan's *lettres de famille*, from 1838 to 1848.

2. These descriptions are taken from "La Poésie des races celtiques," *Essais de morale et de critique* (II, 252). The best critical study of Renan's Celticism is René Galand's *L'Ame celtique de Renan* (See Selected Bibliography).

3. There are very few references in Renan's work to his father; most are to be found in *Ma Sœur Henriette*. The sister was much closer to their father, whose melancholy nature Renan believed she had inherited.

4. Many years later, in his *Conférence sur Marc-Aurèle* (VII, 681), Renan refers to "those [Breton] saints of doubtful orthodoxy." Brittany's record in producing brilliant but suspect (when not downright heretical) religious thinkers or apologists of Christianity is also excellent: Pelagius (fifth-century monk, opposed by Saint Augustine for his heresy in denying original sin), Abelard, Lamennais, Chateaubriand . . . Renan himself (?).

5. His revolt also has a touch of Faust in it. See his letter of Sept. 22, 1845, to Henriette (IX, 792): "There are places when I think in reading it [Goethe's *Faust*] that I am telling my own inner story (*mon histoire intérieure*)."

6. In *Souvenirs d'enfance et de jeunesse* (II, 868), Renan will remind his readers of all the *motifs de cœur et d'intérêt* ("of heart and personal advantage") which might have persuaded him to remain a Christian. Turning Pascal's famous *pensée* upside down, one might devise this Renanian thought: "The reason has its reasons which the heart knows not" (*La raison a ses raisons que le cœur ne connaît point*).

7. Claudel, at the end of the century, referred to the fissure in the prison wall of Positivism which the reading of Rimbaud opened up for him, a promise of escape. Actually, out of fairness to the seminary, we should point out, as Renan did in *Souvenirs*, what he

154

owed in the way of outside influence to the admirable Scholastic method of disputation: knowing the views of unorthodox opponents, stating them forthrightly, and trying to refute them according to reason.

8. I am pleased to find that Professor Jean Pommier, in an article based partly on an unpublished "Examen des marques de vocation" written by Renan while still in seminary in 1845, confirms the impression I derive from the published letters of a calm center in the midst of crisis. See his: "Comment Renan a perdu la foi et quitté le séminaire. Une analyse nouvelle de son drame de conscience," *Le Figaro littéraire*, Oct. 17, 1959, pp. 5-6.

9. I am careful to attribute to Renan "egoism" (self-centeredness) rather than "egotism" (boastfulness or selfishness). "An egoistic man is not necessarily selfish, an egotistic one is" (O.E.D.). The whole vast field of learning in which Renan was to engage saved him from absorption in self of the pettier kind.

Chapter Two

1. *Cahiers de jeunesse* and *Nouveaux Cahiers de jeunesse* were published posthumously in 1906-1907. The *Cahiers* overlap in date of composition with the seminary letters, having been begun in June, 1845. In this chapter I limit myself to the *Cahiers*, for they constitute a source or repertory of ideas to be developed in much greater detail in *L'Avenir de la science*, which I discuss in Chapter 3.

2. *Journal, 1921-1923* (1946), I, 185-186. Du Bos says that the *Cahiers* go "even beyond the intimate journal" (*par-delà même le journal intime*) in sincerity.

3. See Chapter 8.

4. The Biblical reference (*Genesis*, XXXVII, 24) is to the cistern (or receptacle for collecting rain water) into which Joseph was thrown by his brothers before being sold into slavery. The image, I think, is intended to express Renan's storing up of new waters to nourish his thought, perhaps also his having been shorn of the faith which was his birthright.

5. For Lamartine's influence on Renan, see Henri Peyre, "Renan et Lamartine," *Essays in Honor of Albert Feuillerat* (1943), pp. 211-230.

6. The criticism of clarity, taste (*goût*), regularity, the art of "writing well" (*bien écrire*) as hindrances, in France, to the complete expression of thought will remain an important motif in Renan. I shall return to this point in Chapter 9.

7. For further discussion of Renan's views on literary criticism and on Sainte-Beuve, see Henri Peyre, "Ernest Renan, critique littéraire," *PMLA*, XLIV (1929), 288-308, and two articles of mine, "Renan or the Contemptuous Approach to Literature," *Yale French Studies*, II

(1949), 96-104, and "Renan and Sainte-Beuve," *Romantic Review,* XLIV (1953), 127-135.

8. Flaubert does also say, however, that the true "masters" among poets are those who "sum up humanity" (*les vrais maîtres résument l'humanité:* letter to Louise Colet, Oct. 23, 1846). The idea is analogous to Renan's, as is Leconte de Lisle's "effacing" of himself in favor of the larger synthesis of humanity (*Je m'efface, je me synthétise*), a remark of 1845 quoted in Irving Putter's *The Pessimism of Leconte de Lisle* (1961), p. 145.

9. There are excellent discussions of the nineteenth-century dream of total synthesis in Ernst Curtius's *Balzac* (1933), esp. Ch. XII, "L'Oeuvre," and in Léon Emery's *L'Age romantique* (1960). Renan's phrasing is at times very close to that of Hugo in the *Préface de Cromwell* (*il y a du tout dans tout; harmonie des contraires, etc.*)

10. Victor Cousin, professor of philosophy, one of the trio (Guizot and Villemain were the others) of brilliant Sorbonne lecturers around 1830, is best known for his *Cours de philosophie,* first published in 1836. He was extremely active in promoting the study of the history of philosophy and in introducing German philosophy (Hegel above all) into France.

Chapter Three

1. In his 1890 Preface, Renan says he has corrected only the *inadvertences* or *grosses fautes* that he discovered in reading proof (III, 721). Fragments of the manuscript had, in fact, been published much earlier in periodical articles and in other books of his.

2. In a famous sentence, "Literary history is destined to replace in great part the direct reading of works of the human mind" (III, 908), Renan seems to anticipate all too well the cult of literary history associated with Gustave Lanson, the so-called *critique universitaire* which has come under attack recently by "structural critics" in France who consider it nefarious.

3. Despite Renan's comparison of *L'Avenir* (in the same letter evoking the *Discours de la méthode*) to Bacon's *Novum organum.*

4. See *L'Avenir, III,* 757. The phrases are capitalized in the text. Renan will repeat the very wording, with only minor changes, in his *Dialogues philosophiques* (I, 597).

5. These two types of imagery will also recur in *Dialogues philosophiques* (see, e.g., I, 572, 584).

6. Compare Théoctiste in *Dialogues philosophiques* (I, 624): "The medieval idea of some people praying for those who have no time to pray, is very true. The mob labors, some individuals fulfill for it the high functions of life; such is humanity. . . . Some live for all (*Quelques-uns vivent pour tous*). If one tries to change this order, no one will live."

7. "Renan ou l'équation de l'humanité," in his *Aventures de l'esprit* (1954), p. 84. Guéhenno's insight into Renan, in this brilliant essay, is in no way diminished by his admiration for that very different type of genius, Michelet.

Chapter Four

1. *Souvenirs*, II, 766. The word *critique* as Renan uses it here is certainly broad enough to include history.
2. Marc Bloch, *Apologie pour l'histoire ou Métier d'historien* (1949), p. ix. Compare Renan, *Vie de Jésus* (IV, 115), "The Jew . . . brought history into religion" (*Le juif . . . a fait entrer l'histoire dans la religion*).
3. Webster defines the plural, "propylaea," as "the architectural structure forming the entrance to the Acropolis."
4. Renan's second, or Latin, thesis (according to the then French requirement), *De philosophia peripetetica apud Syros,* "traces the Aristotelian philosophy from Alexandria to the Nestorian Syrians, from the Syrians to the Persians and Arabs, and more slightly, from the Arabs to the Schoolmen" (Lewis Mott, *Ernest Renan* [1921], p. 152). *Averroès* continues to be cited in the Encyclopedia Britannica as one of the authoritative works on the subject.
5. See *Cahiers de jeunesse*, IX, 87. Later in the same passage, in fact, Renan refers to the Christians as having understood this type of "life" in believing that "the history of the Church is the history of Jesus Christ continued."
6. See *Préface, L'Avenir de la science*, III, 716.
7. Renan's *Livre de Job*—largely because he contests in part the authenticity of the Biblical work, denies it was divinely inspired, and considers it purely as literature—was his first publication to be placed on the Index Librorum Prohibitorum (Decree of Congregation of Index, Apr. 11, 1859).
8. *Préface, Marc-Aurèle*, V, 740. Pommier questions Renan's retrospective explanation, preferring to believe that the real reason for his plunging *in medias res* was his journey to the Middle East in 1860-1861 and *le prestige de la vision palestinienne* (*Renan d'après des documents inédits* [1923], p. 159).
9. III, 960. See also *Etudes d'histoire religieuse* (VII, 38): "To write the history of a religion, one must no longer believe in it, but one must have believed in it: we understand well only the cult which has aroused in us the first impulse toward the ideal (*le premier élan vers l'idéal*)."

Chapter Five

1. *To the Finland Station, a Study in the Writing and Acting of History* (1940), p. 43.

2. For Renan's position on the Fourth Gospel, see *Préface*, 13th edition, *Vie de Jésus* (IV, 19-21), and Appendix to same edition, "On the Use Which It Is Appropriate to Make of the Fourth Gospel in Writing the Life of Jesus." Renan retracts his belief that John authored this Gospel but continues to claim some historical value for its narrative portions.

3. Renan had already outlined this concept while still at Saint-Sulpice, in his "Essai psychologique sur Jésus-Christ" (May 1845), first published by Jean Pommier in *Revue de Paris*, Sept. 15, 1920. See also, "Les Historiens critiques de Jésus," *Etudes d'histoire religieuse.*

4. *The Life of Jesus* (trans. Olive Wyon, 1933), p. 50. Goguel is severe in his judgment of the work, but admits that Renan did achieve one thing: "He brought forward the problem of the life of Jesus in such a way that henceforward it was impossible to withdraw it from this leading position" (p. 52).

5. An interesting feature of Ch. III ("Education de Jésus"), in light of the discovery of the Dead Sea Scrolls, is Renan's belief that the Essenians represented a movement parallel to that of Jesus, but with no influence upon him (IV, 106-107). In *The Scrolls from the Dead Sea*, (1955), Ch. V, "What Would Renan Have Said?", Edmund Wilson reports his interview with A. Dupont-Sommer, professor of Hebrew at the Sorbonne and present director of the *Corpus Inscriptionum Semiticarum* founded by Renan, and a scholar "conscious of carrying on what may be called the Renanian tradition" (p. 100).

6. Erwin Goodenough, in *The Church in the Roman Empire* (1931), p. 13, speaks of Jesus' "powerful personal magnetism."

7. *Vie de Jésus*, IV, 367: "Which of us, pygmies that we are, could do what has been accomplished by the foolish Saint Francis of Assisi, the hysterical Saint Theresa of Avila? . . . *Les mots de sain et de malade sont tout relatifs.*"

8. See Introduction, *Les Apôtres*, IV, 448 ("The last pages of the *Acts* are the only completely historical pages we have on Christian origins"); 457, with Saint Paul as source, one is *en pleine histoire positive*. Note also the increasing use Renan makes of inscriptions beginning in *Les Apôtres*. He will make even greater use of them in *Histoire du peuple d'Israël.*

9. "There is in fact reason to believe that he was regaining his old idealism through contact with the history of the Jewish people," H. W. Wardman, *Ernest Renan, a Critical Biography* (1964), p. 190.

10. Renan's judgment of Paul seems later to have mellowed somewhat: in "Les Portraits de Saint Paul" (1879), reprinted in *Feuilles détachées*, he persists in believing Paul to have been physically ugly but concludes that he was "one of the strongest and most extraordinary souls who ever existed" (II, 1066).

11. J. W. Thompson and B. J. Holm, in their A *History of Historical Writing* (1942), p. 556, term *Marc-Aurèle* "one of the finest syntheses of Roman and classical civilization ever written."

12. *Essais de morale et de critique*, II, 91. For *Teste David cum Sibylla. O divine comédie!* see *Histoire du peuple d'Israël*, VI, 303, and for further supporting texts, *Préface, Vie de Jésus*, IV, 30-31 (*Le monde est une comédie à la fois infernale et divine*); *L'Eau de Jouvence*, III, 518 (the *grande troupe de comédiens* who act out "what is called history on the world's boards").

13. "Here again Hegel was certainly right; it is not knowing what people did but understanding what they thought that is the proper definition of the historian's task," R. G. Collingwood, *The Idea of History* (1956), p. 115.

14. Renan seems indebted both to the Enlightenment historians, with their view of the historical process as developing by "an immanent necessity in which unreason itself is only a disguised form of reason" (Collingwood, p. 81) and to Hegel's theory of the "cunning of reason" (as described by Collingwood, p. 103).

15. *Préface, Histoire du peuple d'Israël*, VI, 19. Compare H. Stuart Hughes, *History as Art and as Science* (1964), p. 87: the historian, like "other scientists," will "delimit what is possible, what is probable, and what is almost certain."

16. Goodenough, *The Church in the Roman Empire*, p. x. Compare Hughes, pp. 64-65: "The exercise of 'intuition' is at least as important to the historian as his sureness of touch in documentary interpretation."

17. Hughes, p. 103, speaks of the "tone of immediacy and urgency that characterizes all major historical writing." Much of Hughes's analysis of what constitutes the craft of history at its best is applicable to Renan, though he never once mentions his name (See esp. Ch. IV, "The Sweep of the Narrative Line").

18. "History also is a Gospel," Renan quotes from Dom Luigi Tosti, the Benedictine historian of Italian strivings toward nationalism, whom he much admired (*Essais de morale et de critique*, II, 148).

19. See, for the best insight into this great quality of Renan, Charles Péguy's essays, "De la situation faite à l'histoire et à la sociologie dans les temps modernes" and "De la situation faite au parti intellectuel dans le monde moderne," from his *Cahiers de la Quinzaine*, reprinted in *Oeuvres complètes* (1927), vol. III.

Chapter Six

1. Practically all Renan's periodical articles and speeches, fortunately, have been collected in book form. Most of the essays appeared originally in the *Revue des deux mondes* or the *Journal des débats*. Girard and Moncel (see Selected Bibliography) give a complete list-

ing of all these various pieces. For details as to original place and
date of publication (or delivery, where a speech is concerned), I refer
the reader to Girard and Moncel or to the Psichari edition.

2. *Notre siècle ne va ni vers le bien ni vers le mal; il va vers la
médiocrité* (II, 251).

3. *Journal 1889-1939* (1939), pp. 659, 959, 1134.

4. *Ernest Renan, essai de biographie psychologique* (1923), p. 68.

5. For some of Renan's more striking negative remarks on Germany, see: "Nouvelle lettre à M. Strauss" and "La Guerre entre la
France et l'Allemagne," in *La Réforme intellectuelle et morale*, I,
430-432, 456-459; "Rêve de Siffroi" (*L'Eau de Jouvence*, Act IV,
Scene 4: the German ambassador's dream of terrorizing civilian popu-
lations as a means to military victory); the brief but pregnant reference to Germany's cult of obedience and "ungrateful" treatment of
her Jews, in *Souvenirs d'enfance et de jeunesse* (II, 816). The essential text for the prevision of Franco-German co-operation is "Lettre
à un ami d'Allemagne" (*Discours et conférences*).

6. *La Réforme*, "La Guerre entre la France et l'Allemagne," I,
410. Renan's proposed *fédération* also includes another "traditional"
enemy of France, i.e. England. His reference to the United States and
Russia as emerging powers is by no means unique in nineteenth-
century political writing: more detailed prophecies along these lines
had already been made by Hegel, Napoleon, Tocqueville; see Karl
Löwith, *Meaning in History* (1949), pp. 58, 230.

7. See *Préface, Souvenirs d'enfance et de jeunesse* and my discussion of *Caliban* in Chapter 7 ("A Theater of Ideas"). Renan may have
been more sanguine on this point than the much more knowledgeable
Tocqueville, who predicted that freedom of thought would be increasingly restricted in American democracy by the pressure of conformity
to majority opinion.

8. For Renan's most determined attack on pessimism, see *Feuilles
détachées*, "Henri-Frédéric Amiel."

9. *La Réforme*, I, 443. Such remarks represent a palinode of his
earlier attack on French *légèreté*, in *Essais de morale et de critique*
and especially in "La Théologie de Béranger" (*Questions contemporaines*).

10. Or at least not in what C. Wright Mills calls that "uncondi-
tional nationalism," detachment from which is branded by right-
wingers in our own time as "treason"; see *Power, Politics, and People*
(1963), p. 224.

Chapter Seven

1. *Ernest Renan as an Essayist* (1957), pp. 176 ff.

2. This absolutely perfect sentence, one of so many in Renan,
should be quoted in French: *Il se ruait sur la vérité avec la lourde*

impétuosité d'un sanglier: la vérité fugace et légère se détournait, et, faute de souplesse, il la manquait toujours (II, 139).

3. *Renan d'après des documents inédits*, p. 246.

4. "Les Mauvais rêves d'Ernest Renan," *Etudes*, CCLXXXV (1955), 3-14. The reader might also consult my essay, "Renan as Prophet of the European and World Future" (See Selected Bibliography).

5. His arguments are often borrowed from Renan's own, in *La Réforme intellectuelle et morale*.

6. Sir James Frazier, in *The Golden Bough*, takes this legend as the point of departure for his anthropological classic.

7. *L'Abbesse de Jouarre, Avant-Propos de la Première Edition*, III, 611-612. Renan conceives of a work he would have entitled *Dialogues de la dernière nuit*. Dialogues of the Dead had been a classical tradition for centuries; Renan now adds Dialogues of the Dying. What a contrast his *Abbesse de Jouarre* would make with Bernanos's fervently Catholic drama, *Dialogues des Carmélites*, set in the same period!

8. *Qui sait si la vérité n'est pas triste?* (III, 530). Renan was very fond of this phrase. He repeats it in *Préface, Feuilles détachées* (II, 941).

9. Is not Renan expressing what Nietzsche calls "the music in our conscience, the dance in our spirit" (*Beyond Good and Evil*, Gateway Edition [1955], p. 142)? There are more affinities between the two thinkers than Nietzsche's often experssed contempt for Renan would lead us to believe.

10. All these sources are mentioned in the Preface to the Collected Dramas. The reference to Hugo is to his experimental plays of the post-*Burgraves* period. A rapprochement of Renan and Hugo would be enlightening, for they had in common, among other things, a certain sentimentality, the theme of *les religions* versus *la religion*, the facing of the worst in man accompanied by the affirmation of his essential goodness (though Renan is without Hugo's Manichaean strain), the suppression of sin (Renan disbelieves in it while Hugo finally redeems even Satan). Hugo "was an essential member of the Church in whose communion we live [i.e., the invisible Church of believers in humanity]," wrote Renan, in the course of his tribute, "Victor Hugo au lendemain de sa mort," *Feuilles détachées*. (See also my Chap. 2, Note 9.)

11. See Johan Huizinga, *Homo Ludens, a Study of the Play Element in Culture* (1950), p. 149. The whole of Chapter IX ("Play-Forms in Philosophy") throws light on Renan's play of ideas, though he is not mentioned.

12. In his annotated edition of *Caliban* (See Selected Bibliography), Colin Smith brings out very well the topical allusions in the

play, especially the similarity between Caliban and the great Republican leader, Léon Gambetta.

Chapter Eight

1. *Mythes, rêves et mystères* (1957), pp. 29-30. See also Pierre Grimal, "L'Homme et le mythe," in *Mythologies de la Méditerranée au Gange* (1963); for this historian myth is very rarely "gratuitous day-dream" and is in no way essentially opposed to scientific thought, since both myth and science have as their ambition "to explain the world, to render its phenomena intelligible" (pp. 4-5). In this chapter, I use the word "myth" in these positive senses.

2. IX, 1498-1499. "I have lamented with Israel, / I have called upon him who is to come"; "I have seen God in a piece of bread. / This God may be eaten and drunk"; "I struggle against the impossible, / I curse the language of mortals."

3. Renan's possible sources, in addition to *Werther* (1774), are two other "confessional novels," Sainte-Beuve's *Volupté* (1834; mentioned by him, IX, 1514) and *Woldemar* (1779), by the German philosopher Friedrich Jacobi.

4. This was another of Renan's favorite themes: see, e.g., the undated "Les Deux chœurs. Fragment de l'histoire primitive de l'humanité" (IX, 1578-1584).

5. See IX, 1532, "Please God that one day, converted and once again become blind, I may participate in the feast of the pure in heart and commune again with the woman and the child!"; also, composed around the same time, the concluding sentences of *L'Avenir de la science* (III, 1121), "Adieu then, God of my youth! Perhaps you will be that of my deathbed. Adieu; although you have deceived me, I still love you!"

6. For examples of how Renan softens some of the harsher details of Henriette's experience in Syria, see Pommier, *Renan d'après des documents inédits*, Ch. VII, esp. pp. 136-138.

7. Maurras's phrase occurs in his *Pages littéraires choisies* (1922), p. 141. A variation on the "symbol and image" theme, *Tout n'est ici-bas que symbole et que songe* ("symbol and dream") occurs twice in Renan's work: *Souvenirs d'enfance et de jeunesse* (*Prière sur l'Acropole*), II, 759; Dedication, *Saint Paul*, IV, 708.

8. Compare Baudelaire: *Tous les littérateurs ont horreur de la littérature à de certains moments.*

9. See Pommier, "Comment fut composée la 'Prière sur l'Acropole'," *Revue de Paris*, V (1923), 437-447, and his edition of *Souvenirs* (See Selected Bibliography), pp. xlv ff.

10. See Chapter 1, and present chapter, "Early Poetic and Novelistic Fragments."

11. *La Prière sur l'Acropole et ses mystères* (See Selected Bibliography), pp. 7-8.

12. Like so many Renanian themes, this one is already contained in *L'Avenir de la science,* but is stated there in a much more solemn context; see III, 1121, "I have been formed by the Church, I owe it what I am, and will never forget that" (*J'ai été formé par l'Eglise, je lui dois ce que je suis, et ne l'oublierai jamais*).

13. *Literary Reviews and Essays,* ed. Albert Mordell (1957), p. 42.

14. II, 939. For this collection, Renan found one of his loveliest titles, *Detached Leaves,* suggesting at least a triple meaning: his life's autumn fading into winter (the leaves have already fallen); the calm with which he views the enjoyable spectacle coming to an end; and finally, pages of his work for which he claimed no major importance (*ces feuilles, souvent légères*). Written at the suggestion of his publisher, Calmann-Lévy, who had asked him for more anecdotes about Brittany (*bretonneries*), the book adds nothing essential to his portrait in *Souvenirs,* but is unfailingly readable and does in fact contain a number of important critical and philosophical essays (esp. "Henri-Frédéric Amiel" and "Examen de conscience philosophique").

15. *The Autobiography of William Butler Yeats,* Doubleday Anchor Book (1958), p. 84.

16. *Design and Truth in Autobiography* (1960), p. 56. In the remaining pages of this chapter, I have quoted a number of Roy Pascal's other phrases, all from this single book.

Chapter Nine

1. *Paroles de Renan à un adolescent* (1930), p. 21. (See Selected Bibliography.)

2. Quoted in *The Letters of Robert Frost to Louis Untermeyer,* ed. Louis Untermeyer (1964).

3. Jean Pommier, *Renan d'après des documents inédits,* p. 359.

4. *L'Oeuvre scientifique d'Ernest Renan,* p. 50.

5. *The Spirit of the Age* (Doubleday Dolphin Book, n.d.), p. 99 (from the essay on Lord Byron).

Selected Bibliography

PRIMARY SOURCES

Original Editions

(Place of publication is Paris)

L'Abbesse de Jouarre. Calmann-Lévy, 1886. Philosophical drama.

L'Antéchrist. Michel Lévy, 1873. Fourth vol. of *Histoire des origines du christianisme.*

Les Apôtres. Michel Lévy, 1866. Second vol. of *Origines.*

L'Avenir de la science. Calmann-Lévy, 1890.

Averroès et l'averroïsme, essai historique. Durand, 1852.

Cahiers de jeunesse (1845-1846). Calmann-Lévy, 1906. Posthumous.

Caliban, suite de la Tempête. Calmann-Lévy, 1878. Philosophical drama.

Le Cantique des cantiques, traduit de l'hébreu, avec une étude sur le plan, l'âge et le caractère du poème. Michel Lévy, 1860.

Conférences d'Angleterre. Rome et le christianisme. Marc-Aurèle. Calmann-Lévy, 1880. Hibbert Lectures (London).

Correspondance (1846-1892). 2 vols. Calmann-Lévy, 1926-1928. Posthumous. Exclusive of letters to Henriette, mother, and Berthelot.

Correspondance de MM Renan et Berthelot (1847-1892). Calmann-Lévy, 1898. Posthumous.

De l'origine du langage. Joubert, 1848.

Dialogues et fragments philosophiques. Calmann-Lévy, 1876.

Discours et conférences. Calmann-Lévy, 1887.

Drames philosophiques. Calmann-Lévy, 1888. Collective edition of four philosophical dramas.

L'Eau de Jouvence, suite de Caliban. Calmann-Lévy, 1881.

L'Ecclésiaste, traduit de l'hébreu, avec une étude sur l'âge et le caractère du livre. Calmann-Lévy, 1882.

L'Eglise chrétienne. Calmann-Lévy, 1879. Sixth vol. of *Origines.*

Essais de morale et de critique. Michel Lévy, 1859.

Etudes d'histoire religieuse. Michel Lévy, 1857.

Les Evangiles et la seconde génération chrétienne. Calmann-Lévy, 1877. Fifth vol. of *Origines.*

Feuilles détachées, faisant suite aux Souvenirs d'enfance et de jeunesse. Calmann-Lévy, 1892.

Fragments intimes et romanesques. Calmann-Lévy, 1914. Posthumous.

Henriette Renan. Souvenir pour ceux qui l'ont connue. Claye, 1862. Limited printing (100 copies).

Histoire du peuple d'Israël. Calmann-Lévy, 1887. 5 vols. Vols. 4 and 5 published posthumously in 1893.

Histoire générale et système comparé des langues sémitiques. Imprimerie nationale, 1855.

Lettres du séminaire (1838-1846). Calmann-Lévy, 1902. Posthumous.

Lettres intimes d'Ernest Renan et Henriette Renan (1842-1843). Calmann-Lévy, 1896. Posthumous.

Le Livre de Job, traduit de l'hébreu, avec une étude sur l'âge et le caractère du poème. Michel Lévy, 1858.

Ma Sœur Henriette. Calmann-Lévy, 1895. Posthumous. Reprint of *Henriette Renan* (1862).

Marc-Aurèle et la fin du monde antique. Calmann-Lévy, 1882. Seventh vol. of *Origines.*

Mélanges d'histoire et de voyages. Calmann-Lévy, 1878.

Mélanges religieux et historiques. Calmann-Lévy, 1904. Posthumous.

Nouveaux cahiers de jeunesse (1846). Calmann-Lévy, 1907. Posthumous.

Nouvelles études d'histoire religieuse. Calmann-Lévy, 1884.

Nouvelles lettres intimes d'Ernest Renan et Henriette Renan (1846-1850). Calmann-Lévy, 1923. Posthumous.

Le Prêtre de Némi. Calmann-Lévy, 1885. Philosophical drama.

Questions contemporaines. Michel Lévy, 1868.

La Réforme intellectuelle et morale. Michel Lévy, 1871.

Saint Paul. Michel Lévy, 1869. Third vol. of *Origines.*

Souvenirs d'enfance et de jeunesse. Calmann-Lévy, 1883.

Vie de Jésus. Michel Lévy, 1863. First vol. of *Origines.* Revised edition (13th), 1864. Abridged or popular edition, 1864.

Edition of Complete Works

Oeuvres complètes, ed., Henriette Psichari. 10 vols. Paris: Calmann-Lévy, 1947-1961. Indexes (lacking in older editions), translations of quotations in foreign languages, and (for vols. 3-7, major historical works) bibliographies of sources used, enhance the value of this edition, though there are few editorial notes.

Scholarly or Annotated Editions

Caliban, suite de la Tempête, ed., Colin Smith. Manchester: Manchester Univ. Press, 1954. (French Classics.)

Prière sur l'Acropole, ed., Eugène Vinaver and T. B. L. Webster. Manchester: Manchester Univ. Press, 1934. (French Classics.)

La Réforme intellectuelle et morale, ed., P. E. Charvet. Cambridge: Cambridge University Press, 1950.

Souvenirs d'enfance et de jeunesse, ed., Irving Babbitt. Boston, New York, Chicago: D. C. Heath, 1902.

Souvenirs d'enfance et de jeunesse, ed., Jean Pommier. Paris: Armand Colin, 1959. (Bibliothèque de Cluny.) The most copiously annotated.

Souvenirs d'enfance et de jeunesse, ed., Gilbert Guisan. Lausanne: Editions Rencontre, 1961.

Editions of Selected Passages

Pages choisies. Paris: Calmann-Lévy, c. 1890. Extracts chosen by Renan, with emphasis on *L'Avenir de la science* and *Souvenirs.*

Pages choisies, ed., Philippe Van Tieghem. Paris: Hachette, 1952. (Classiques illustrés Vaubourdolle.)

Les Sciences de la nature et les sciences historiques. L'Avenir de la science, ed., Ira Wade. Princeton: Princeton Univ. Press, 1944. (Princeton Texts in Literature and the History of Thought.)

Souvenirs d'enfance et de jeunesse. Ma Sœur Henriette, Feuilles détachées, ed., Bernard Lalande. Paris: Larousse, n.d. (Classiques Larousse.)

Selected English Translations

Brother and Sister. A Memoir and the Letters of Ernest and Henriette Renan, trans., Lady M. Lloyd. London: Heinemann, 1896.

Caliban. A Philosophical Drama Continuing the Tempest of William Shakespeare, trans., E. G. Vickery. New York: Shakespeare Press, and London: Kegan Paul, 1896. (Publications of Shakespeare Society of New York, No. 9.)

The Future of Science, trans., Albert Vandam and C. B. Pitman. London: Chapman, 1891.

History of the People of Israel, trans., J. H. Allen and Mrs. E. W. Lattimer. 5 vols. Boston: Little, Brown, c. 1895.

Lectures on the Influence of the Institutions, Thought and Culture of Rome on Christianity and the Development of the Catholic Church, trans., Charles Beard. London: Williams and Norgate, 1880. (Hibbert Lectures.)

The Life of Jesus. New York: Modern Library, c. 1955.

The Origins of Christianity, trans., William Hutchison. 7 vols. London: W. Scott, 1897-1904.

Philosophical Dialogues and Fragments, trans., Râs Bihârî Mukharjî. London: Trübner, 1883.

The Poetry of the Celtic Races, trans., William Hutchison. New York: Collier, 1910. (Harvard Classics, vol. XXXII).

Recollections of My Youth, trans., C. B. Pitman. London: Chapman and Hall, 1883.

SECONDARY SOURCES

ALBALAT, ANTOINE. *La Vie de Jésus d'Ernest Renan*. Paris: Malfère, 1933. Considered as a *grand événement littéraire*.

BABBITT, IRVING. *Masters of Modern French Criticism*. Boston and New York: Houghton Mifflin, 1912. Reprinted from Introduction to his edition of *Souvenirs* (See Primary Sources). Best essay on Renan in English.

BOULENGER, JACQUES. *Renan et ses critiques*. Paris: Editions du siècle, 1925. Vigorous defense.

BRANDES, GEORG. *Eminent Authors of the Nineteenth Century*. New York: Crowell, 1886. Good portrait by Danish critic who interviewed Renan.

————. "Ernest Renan as a Dramatist," *International Quarterly*, X (1904), 71-91. Insights into virtues and limitations of Renan's theater.

BRUNET, GABRIEL. *Evocations littéraires*. Paris: Editions Prométhée, 1930. Perceptive essay on Renan's thought and style, and Appendix proposing his *esprit universel* as antidote for overspecialization of our age.

CHADBOURNE, RICHARD M. *Ernest Renan as an Essayist*. Ithaca: Cornell Univ. Press, 1957.

————. "Renan and Sainte-Beuve," *Romanic Review*, XLIV (1953), 127-135.

————. "Renan as Prophet of the European and World Future," *American Society of Legion of Honor Magazine*, XXII (1951), 299-309.

————. "Renan or the Contemptuous Approach to Literature," *Yale French Studies*, II (1949), 96-104.

CHAIX-RUY, JULES. *Ernest Renan*. Paris and Lyon: Emmanuel Vitte, 1956. Interesting, though not fully successful, attempt to interpret Renan as concealing "existential anguish."

CRESSON, ANDRE. *Ernest Renan, sa vie, son œuvre, avec un exposé de sa philosophie*. Paris: Presses Universitaires de France, 1949. Useful summary of thought, but somewhat oversimplified. Contains extracts from philosophical works.

DARMESTETER, JAMES. "Ernest Renan," *The New World*, II (1893), 401-433. Valuable portrait of scholar and teacher by eminent Orientalist who knew him. Reprinted in author's *Selected Essays*, trans., Helen and Morris Jastrow. Boston and New York: Houghton Mifflin, 1895.

DUBREUIL, LEON. *Rosmapamon*. Paris: Ariane, 1946. Renan *vieillard* in his Breton summer home.

DUSSAUD, RENE. *L'Oeuvre scientifique d'Ernest Renan*. Paris: Guethner, 1951. Surveys Renan's learned works. On the whole favorable. Author a distinguished Orientalist.

GALAND, RENE. *L'Ame celtique de Renan*. New Haven: Yale Univ. Press, and Paris: Presses Universitaires de France, 1959. Best available study of Celtic theme in Renan's life and works.

GIRARD, HENRI and HENRI MONCEL. *Bibliographie des œuvres d'Ernest Renan*. Paris: Presses Universitaires de France, 1923. Indispensable listing of manuscripts and primary sources.

GUEHENNO, JEAN. *Aventures de l'esprit*. Paris: Gallimard, 1954. Superb essay, critical yet sympathetic: "Renan ou l'équation de l'humanité."

GUERARD, ALBERT. *French Prophets of Yesterday. A Study of Religious Thought under the Second Empire*. London and Leipzig: T. Fisher Unwin, 1913. Excellent, both for pages on Renan and as background reading.

GUISAN, GILBERT. *Ernest Renan et l'art d'écrire*. Geneva: Droz, 1962. Good study of style, but a more thorough one is still needed.

LAGRANGE, M.-J. *La Vie de Jésus d'après Renan*. Paris: Lecoffre, 1923. Criticism from point of view of orthodox Catholic exegesis.

LASSERRE, PIERRE. *Renan et nous*. Paris: Grasset, 1923. Good brief assessment.

————. *La Jeunesse d'Ernest Renan. Histoire de la crise religieuse au XIXe siècle*. 3 vols. Paris: Garnier and Calmann-Lévy, 1925-1932. Places crisis on broad philosophical background, probes into its significance for modern men. Good, though notorious for digressions.

LEVY-BRUHL, LUCIEN. *History of Modern Philosophy in France*. Chicago: Open Court, 1899. Essay on Renan and Taine, good analysis and criticism of Renan's philosophy. Stresses pseudo-skepticism.

MONOD, GABRIEL. *Renan, Taine, et Michelet. Les Maîtres de l'histoire*. Paris: Calmann-Lévy, 1894. One of best assessments of historical work; excellent moral portrait.

MOTT, LEWIS F. *Ernest Renan*. New York and London: Appleton Century, 1921. Best book in English to consult for biographical facts and summaries of works.

NEFF, EMERY. *The Poetry of History. The Contribution of Literature and Literary Scholarship to the Writing of History since Voltaire.* New York: Columbia Univ. Press, 1947. Good background reading, especially chapter relating Renan to Jacob Burckhardt and John Richard Green; argues for permanent value of Renan's approach to writing of history.

PEYRE, HENRI. "Ernest Renan critique littéraire," *PMLA,* XLIV (1929), 288-308. Defines original contribution and limitations of Renan as literary critic.

POMMIER, JEAN. *La Pensée religieuse de Renan.* Paris: Rieder, 1925. Excellent analysis of Renan's religious and philosophical thought, with valuable compendium of his major terms in this field.

————. *Renan d'après des documents inédits.* Paris: Perrin, 1923. Pioneer work in establishing authoritative biography. Remains one of most reliable general studies in French.
(I have mentioned only what I consider the two most important contributions, among many fine articles and books of Pommier, who ranks with Henriette Psichari as the leading French *renaniste.*)

PSICHARI, HENRIETTE. *Des jours et des hommes (1890-1961).* Paris: Grasset, 1962. Reminiscences of Renan in last years (against background of time), by his granddaughter.

————. *La Prière sur l'Acropole et ses mystères.* Paris: Editions du Centre National de Recherche Scientifique, 1956. Exhaustive and enlightening study of this famous text.

————. *Renan d'après lui-même.* Paris: Plon, 1937. Superb *biographie spirituelle;* utilizes journal of Cornélie Renan and presents revealing *pensées inédites.* Author sympathetic to Renan, but neither her scholarship nor her critical sense shows any bias.

————. *Renan et la guerre de 70.* Paris: Albin Michel, 1947. Supplements preceding work, with emphasis on political thought. Convincing defense of Renan's conduct in Franco-Prussian War and in post-war years.

PUTTER, IRVING. *The Pessimism of Leconte de Lisle.* Berkeley and Los Angeles: Univ. of California Press, 1961. Many references to Renan, especially in Part II, "The Work and the Time." Valuable general views on spirit of Renan's generation.

ROLLAND, ROMAIN. *Paroles de Renan à un adolescent.* Paris: Editions de la Belle Page, 1930. A famous author's visit as youth to Renan in 1886 and testimony to his power over the younger generation at that time.

SAINTE-BEUVE, CHARLES AUGUSTIN. *Nouveaux Lundis.* Paris: Michel Lévy, 1863-1870. 13 vols. Vol. II contains two articles (1862) on Renan's first essay collections, learned works, and Biblical translations. Vol. VI contains article (1863) on *Vie de Jésus*. On the whole, very shrewd and perceptive criticism.

SARTON, GEORGE. *The Life of Science. Essays in the History of Civilization*. New York: Schuman, 1948. High praise for Renan's understanding of the scientific point of view, by a leading historian of science.

SCHWEITZER, ALBERT. *The Quest of the Historical Jesus. A Critical Study of Its Progress from Reimarus to Wrede*. New York: Macmillan, 1948. (Translation from original German work of 1906.) Situates Renan in broad current of developing Biblical criticism; generally very severe in judgment of *Vie de Jésus*.

SEAILLES, GABRIEL. *Ernest Renan. Essai de biographie psychologique*. Paris: Perrin, 1895. One of best critical analyses of Renan's philosophical thought, although isolates thinker too much from artist.

SMITH, COLIN. "The Fictionalist Element in Renan's Thought," *French Studies*, IX (1955), 30-41. Good essay on Renan as precursor of philosophy of "useful lie" or "as if" (i.e. to act "as if" God existed), developed by Vaihinger.

SOLTAU, ROGER. *French Political Thought in the Nineteenth Century*. New Haven: Yale Univ. Press, 1931. Brief but good summary of Renan's politics, against broad background.

STRAUSS, GASTON. *La Politique de Renan, suivie d'une étude sur les candidatures de 1869 et 1879 d'après des notes et des documents inédits*. Paris: Grevin, 1909. Most complete study on subject to date.

VAN TIEGHEM, PHILIPPE. *Renan*. Paris: Hachette, 1948. Good introduction and comprehensive view, though not especially critical or original. Part of series: "Les Grands Ecrivains Français."

VIRTANEN, REINO. *Marcelin Berthelot. A Study of a Scientist's Public Role*. Lincoln: Univ. of Nebraska Press, 1965. (Univ. of Nebraska Studies: New Series, No. 31.) Carefully nuanced pages (12-22) on "Berthelot and Renan."

WARDMAN, H. W. *Ernest Renan. A Critical Biography*. London: Univ. of London (Athlone) Press, 1964. Excellent general study, stressing concept of "hidden God" in Renan's work.

———. "'L'Esprit de finesse' and Style in Renan," *Modern Language Review*, LIX (1964), 215-224. Perceptive, especially on symbolism of Greek and Celtic myths for Renan.

———. "Imagery and Myth in Renan," *French Studies*, VII (1953), 197-213. Interesting study of several key images (especially those relating to embryogeny) recurring in Renan's philosophical thought.

WEILER, MAURICE. *La Pensée de Renan*. Grenoble: Bordas Frères, 1945. Good introduction to Renan's thought.

WILSON, EDMUND. *To the Finland Station. A Study in the Writing and Acting of History*. New York: Harcourt Brace, 1940. Situates Renan in the "decline of the revolutionary tradition"; considers him an incomparable master of the history of "man's formulated ideas."

Index